D1368009

The Last Things

REGIS MARTIN

The Last Things

Death
Judgment
Hell
Heaven

IGNATIUS PRESS   SAN FRANCISCO

Cover art:
Tympanum showing Last Judgment
Abbey Ste. Foy. Conques, France
Scala/Art Resource, NY

Cover design by Roxanne Mei Lum

ISBN 0–89870–662–9
Library of Congress catalogue number 97–76855
Printed in the United States of America ∞

In memory of my mother,
Elizabeth Naomi Martin,
who first introduced me
to the Last Things

Question: What are the Four Last Things to be ever remembered?

Answer: The Four Last Things to be ever remembered are Death, Judgment, Hell and Heaven.
— *The Penny Catechism*

Prayer for a Good Death

O merciful Christ, omnipotent judge of the universe and all creatures within it, I know that someday I shall stand before you to render an account of all that I am and have done. Grant me the grace to gird my mind and will to face that fearful summons; to fortify myself at all times with the grace of a good life; to persevere to the end amid the holy ministrations of Mother Church. Preserve me and all your children from a sudden and unprovided death. Send your angels and saints to hover about us at the last, lest the Evil One entice us to despair of your mercy and protection. Saint Joseph, Patron of a Good Death, be with me in my final agony; give me comfort and solace in the midst of pain, to long for and await my Redeemer's deliverance. I ask you this through Christ our Lord. Amen.

Contents

Preface

"Well, Harriet, what do we do next? I think we've seen every-thing now."

It was more than ten years ago in Rome when, coming out of a cappuchino bar, I overheard the two of them talking on the sidewalk. It was too good to pass up (and I thought *I'd* seen everything!). Here were a prize pair of blooming innocents from the New World, at the end of their first full day in Rome, whose charms, as every artist will tell you, are akin to falling in love, and wouldn't you just know it, they'd already picked the place clean.

I resisted asking any of the usual questions, the ones whose answers are all too easily turned to ridicule. "Oh, the Colosseum? Sure, we've seen it. Just great. When's it gonna be finished?" Or the exchange that, so help me, I once overheard in the depths of the catacombs of Saint Domitilla between two Americans of indeterminate age, neither of whom could be certain whether the construction date on the tunnels was B.C. or A.D. I kept my own counsel then; this time a droll impulse took hold, and I spoke.

Had they seen, I asked, Santa Maria della Concezione? No, they hadn't. Well, it's quite extraordinary, you know: a Capuchin church, located right at the bottom of Via Veneto . . .

"Oh, now, we've certainly been there!"

It was all that I'd feared. Via Veneto, yes. Everyone's been there. Rome's most glittering showcase, the place where the rich and famous once disported themselves and where, alas nowadays, only tourists, armed with credit cards and cameras, abound. Yes, they'd been to Via Veneto. In fact, their tour was staying nearby, and so they'd seen all the sights: Harry's Bar, the restaurants replete with American fast food, the boutiques, the discos, and all the news they had gone two whole days without.

"What's so special about this Santa place, huh?"

"It is full of dead men's bones", I said. "Try and think of it as the surprise stop on the tour. You know, the place they'd forgotten to schedule."

They left pretty quickly after that, muttering and shaking their heads in disbelief. How long, I could just hear him telling Harriet, how long has *he* been left out in the sun?

I can't help it: Santa Maria della Concezione is just about my favorite place in the whole world. Indeed, were I to have guided their tour bus through the Eternal City, I'd have driven straight from the airport to this splendid house of the dead, where clever Capuchin friars have piled high their crypt (four subterranean chapels, no less!) with the skeletal remains of four thousand souls who were once like thee and me.

Such a hugely funny joke, too, to have situated the whole overflowing *Memento mori* right at the foot of fashionable Via Veneto, as if to serve notice on the worldly that they too shall come to an end. Admittedly, Santa Maria della Concezione hasn't any of the sparkle and glitter that so beguile the visitor, ineluctably drawn to *La Dolce Vita* further up the street. But unlike the fleshpots, of which, let's face it, after twenty or so minutes the palate wearies (it is, after all, only the allure of the veneer that arrests the senses), one is free to wander down to the Capuchin crypt and there begin a most lively scrutiny of

Death. Where one confronts firsthand the stark, unmediated truth about oneself, and others, and the world. The truth that all is vanity, destined soon enough to wither like the grass.

"Do tell me what you think of life", a woman asked of Henry James. "I think", replied the master, "it is a predicament which precedes death." The first of the Four Last Things ever to be remembered, Death is a subject about which we can never say enough. And when we begin to think wisely and well of Death, it soon follows that the other three—namely, Judgment, Hell, and Heaven—are very likely to invite fruitful inquiry as well. Even tourists would do well to remember the Last Things. For it is not well—no, not even for tourists, whose vacation lives suggest something of the character of all lives (a state of parenthesis between time and eternity)—to forget the End.

I offer these reflections, for whatever they may be worth, in memory of my mother, who first awakened in me an interest in the Last Things.

On the Last Things

Try to imagine the one thing in this world that is most worth knowing—by everyone. The thing that is most worth having. Something the sheer longing for which could never be dismissed merely as a function of time or space, tribe or temperament. Is there a sentient being around who has not felt it, wondered about it, made some effort to obtain it? Could it have something to do with the final outcome of our lives? Or the lives of those whom we love? Lives no longer with us but lost, whom we long once more to see, to be with. What does Christianity offer us in this regard? Has the Church anything distinctive to say about it? And if so, can it assuage this most deep and persisting of human hungers?

The answers to these questions, and a clutch of others besides, are to be found in the Church's doctrine of the Last Things. *Eschatology,* which is a term deriving from the Greek word *eschata,* meaning "outcomes" or "ends", is very simply the fruit of the Church's most profound reflection on the meaning of Death, Judgment, Hell, and Heaven (also Purgatory, Limbo, the Second Coming of Christ, and the End or Transfiguration of the World).

Traditionally referred to as the *Four Last Things,* these are the mysteries that bear most directly on the final section of the Creed, namely, "the resurrection of the body, and life everlasting", the loftiest realities to which Christian belief may be expected to aspire. "We seek the city that is to come", declares the author of the Letter to the Hebrews.[1] "I am the resurrection and the life", says Jesus. "He who believes in me, though he die, yet shall he live."[2]

But what a strangely perverse silence fills the air the moment the subject is brought up! Is it not matter for astonishment that while all the ancient peoples incessantly reflected on the nature of the next world, having wisely intuited the impermanence of this passing one, hardly any self-respecting modern appears the least bit interested in the "hereafter"? How seldom, for example, modern man thinks of death, an event that, after all, represents the real point of entry into eternity. *Respice finem,* which means "look to the end", is an ancient pagan motto whose message the Christian religion early on embraced. Indeed, Jesus himself enjoined his disciples to watch and wait, mindful of the End: "Therefore you also must be ready; for the Son of man is coming at an hour you do not expect."[3] However, for most self-styled, enlightened folk, it is hardly the thing to which they care to look at the moment. (The irony, to be sure, is that by the time they finally do turn their minds to the end, it will very likely be the End.) "Humankind cannot bear very much reality", says T. S. Eliot.[4]

In that wonderful Edwardian saga *The Man of Property,* written by John Galsworthy, revealing, among other failings of the Forsyte family, a quite impenetrable complacency about almost everything, one reads the following description of this

---

[1] Heb 13:14.

[2] Jn 11:25.

[3] Mt 24:44.

[4] T. S. Eliot, *Four Quartets* (New York: Harcourt, Brace and World, 1943), p. 14.

"upper middle-class family in full plumage": "When a Forsyte was engaged, married, or born, the Forsytes were present; when a Forsyte died—but no Forsyte had as yet died; they did not die; death being contrary to their principles, they took precautions against it, the instinctive precautions of highly vitalized persons who resent encroachments on their property."[5]

Given the extent of modern man's flight from death, from the "hereafter", one has got to ask in all seriousness whether the human hunger for Heaven has become some sort of vestigial organ. Is it possible for the wings of the human spirit to atrophy for want of use? Nowadays to speak of man's pilgrim status, of his promised homeland in Heaven, of the travail of the world and hope for life beyond the grave, is to invite a blank stare of stupefaction among the many for whom eternity has lost all attraction. Of course, such silence about the End exacts a heavy price. We instinctively know the last act will prove bloody, however pleasant the intervening play. None of us, including the most fatuous of the Forsytes, is exempt from that final nightfall, through the silence of which we shall all someday pass. Alone, we shall pass through the door of Death, which admits only one at a time; we've all been scheduled to go through it. "Someday", Karl Barth writes, "a company of men will process out to a churchyard and lower a coffin and everyone will go home; but one will not come back, and that will be me. The seal of death will be that they will bury me as a thing that is superfluous and disturbing in the land of the living."[6]

.

5 John Galsworthy, *The Man of Property* (New York: Charles Scribner's Sons, 1922), pp. 3, 4.
6 Karl Barth, *Dogmatics in Outline* (London: SCM Press, 1949), pp. 117–18.

Yes, silence, denial, and flight from man's finitude exact a fearful price in the end. "They throw earth over your head and it is finished forever", reports Pascal. (Which is precisely why the author of the *Pensées* adds, "We run heedlessly into the abyss after putting something in front of us to stop us seeing it."[7] We are, says Eliot, "distracted from distraction by distraction."[8])

In any case, eschatological forgetfulness, especially on the part of Christians, will simply force the world to look elsewhere for information and consolation about the End. When men cease to hear the truth about Death or eternal life from Christians, the truth that it is their chief business to dispense, they will not blunder forth like nihilists believing nothing. No, they will more than likely hear and believe anything. Even nonsense is preferable to nihilism. If no one gets out alive, if death is an ambush necessarily awaiting us all, then who among us will not stoop to make even the silliest and most aberrant provision for it?

"For to act in aberration", writes Whittaker Chambers, "is at least more like living than to die of futility, or even to live in that complacency which is futility's idiot twin. We all know those grand aberrations of our time. We have plenty of names for them. . . . But all the aberrations have one common cause, and point, in the end, in one direction."[9] And that direction, of course, is death, despair. " 'The one essential condition of

---

[7] Blaise Pascal, *Pensées* (New York: Penguin Books, 1966), p. 82. "Being unable to cure death, wretchedness and ignorance, men have decided, in order to be happy, not to think about such things." Ibid., p. 66.

[8] Eliot, *Four Quartets,* p. 17.

[9] See William F. Buckley, Jr., editor, *Did You Ever See a Dream Walking? American Conservative Thought in the Twentieth Century* (Indianapolis

human existence'", Chambers quotes Stefan Trofimovitch, a character in Dostoevsky's *The Possessed,*

> "is that man should always be able to bow down before something infinitely great. If men are deprived of the infinitely great, they will not go on living and will die of despair." It is for this that we crave reality.... "I want to know why," Sherwood Anderson asked. I want to know why. It is for this we seek a little height, and because of this we do not feel it too high a price to pay if we cannot reach it crawling through a lifetime on our hands and knees, as a wounded man sometimes crawls from a battlefield, if only so as not to die as one more corpse among so many corpses.[10]

As Dr. Johnson used to say, nothing so wonderfully concentrates the mind as the knowledge that a man is to be hanged in a fortnight. Who wants to go to his own hanging unprepared?

In the face of death, then, that ineluctable irruption we cannot finally postpone, two salutary truths emerge for our consideration. The first, of course, is the reminder that here begin the things that come last, so pray do not put off thinking about them. Defer the thought as long as you please; the thing itself will come in any case. Why not attend to it now? "Men

---

and New York: Bobbs-Merrill, 1970), p. 487. "And if the old paths no longer lead to a reality that enables men to act with meaning, if the paths no longer seem to lead anywhere — have become a footworn, trackless maze, or, like Russian roads, end after a few miles of ambitious pavement leading nowhere but into bottomless mud and swallowing distance — men will break new paths, though they must break their hearts to do it. They will burst out somewhere, even if such bursting-out takes the form of aberration. For to act in aberration ... "

10 Ibid., pp. 486–87.

shun the thought of death as sad," writes Archbishop Fenelon, "but death will only be sad to those who have no thought of it. It must come sooner or later, and then he who has refused to see the truth in life will be forced to face it in death."[11] Is not the decisive Socratic maxim "the unexamined life is not worth living", which countless first-year philosophy students have had to memorize, really nothing more than an extended meditation on death? Without pushing it as far as, say, Plotinus, who hesitated even to give out his address, so much did he hate being in the body, is it not the case that the care of the soul, which is central to man, requires constant reference to the fact and event of death? "We should remember", says Cardinal Newman, "that this life is scarcely more than an accident of our being—that it is no part of ourselves, who are immortal; that we are immortal spirits, independent of time and space, and that this life is a sort of outward stage, on which we act for a time, and which is only sufficient and only intended to answer the purpose of trying whether we will serve God or no."[12] It makes all the difference in the world, says Pascal, "if it is certain that we shall not be here for long, and uncertain whether we shall be here even one hour".[13] *Respice finem* indeed.

Under the circumstances, those who saunter along such a stage, supposing its duration to be forever, will be greatly surprised when, at the last curtain call, the stage and all its props are swept completely away. Death will have proven to

[11] See Barry Ulanov, editor, *Death: A Book of Preparation and Consolation* (New York: Sheed and Ward, 1959), pp. 37–38.

[12] John Henry Newman, *The Heart of Newman,* a synthesis arranged by Erich Przywara, S.J. (San Francisco: Ignatius Press, 1997), p. 297.

[13] Pascal, *Pensées,* p. 81.

be a startling and salutary reminder in helping them overcome the illusion of the world's finality.

So here begin the things that come last. And, point two, here begin the things that will forever last. What have we to do with the allurements of a passing world when, already baptized into the world to come, we cannot belong to this one? Why be anxious about duration or delight in this world when our hearts belong to another? And if everything there is arranged to meet our deepest longings, to quench our most ardent and immortal thirsts, why tarry in the antechamber of joy? "To those who live by faith," says Newman,

> everything they see speaks of that future world; the very glories of nature, the sun, moon, and stars, and the richness and the beauty of the earth, are as types and figures witnessing and teaching the invisible things of God. All that we see is destined one day to burst forth into a heavenly bloom, and to be transfigured into immortal glory. Heaven at present is out of sight, but in due time, as snow melts and discovers what it lay upon, so will this visible creation fade away before those greater splendours which are behind it, and on which at present it depends.[14]

Thus, as Eliot announces in *Four Quartets,* "In my end is my beginning."[15]

When we ponder the meaning of such realities, literally, the Last Things ever to be remembered, we are engaged in an essential exercise that bears on the whole content of Christian hope. And hope is an enormously important, if widely neglected and misunderstood, virtue; to enter upon the study and practice of it will lead one to the heart of the Christian mystery.

[14] Newman, *Heart of Newman,* pp. 298–99.
[15] Eliot, *Four Quartets,* p. 32.

Nothing more sharply distinguishes one's membership in the Body of Christ. Put it this way: the perspective of Catholic belief is one that not only looks at the past, reposing its confidence upon the person and promise of Christ, but also gazes expectantly into the future, venturing all on the Christ who awaits us at the last. We do this, notwithstanding the data of human finitude and Death, because on the strength of our Catholic faith we trust in the eventuality of things to configure themselves more and more mysteriously to Christ. Saint Augustine put it well: "Christ realized what is still a hope for us. We do not see that for which we hope. But we are the body of that head in whom what we expect became reality."[16] With Christ the whole fabled Kingdom of God has finally entered the world, however obscured by the darkening mist of faith. Not to mention the infinitely darker obscurities thrown up by sin. Faith assures us that at the End, on the far side of the grave, the Risen and Triumphant Lord will reveal his glory and power. The hidden and eschatological character of time and history remain in Christ's hands, and so already they bear the stamp and cachet of his being: "The good word of God and the powers of the world to come"[17] have been planted deep in his life and the lives of those annealed in hope, baptized into his Body, the Church.

Another way of putting it is to say that present and future time are really two nondetachable aspects of the same time, the same moment, which is Christic time, the very *kairos* of the Risen Lord. It is what Eliot, in a luminous image, calls "the still point of the turning world". The mystic point where, he says, "past and future are gathered". Except for the point,

---

[16] Quoted in *The Church's Confession of Faith: A Catholic Catechism for Adults* (San Francisco: Ignatius Press, 1987), p. 328.
[17] Heb 6:5.

the still point, "there would be no dance, and there is only the dance."[18]

> The hint half guessed, the gift half
> understood, is Incarnation.
> Here the impossible union
> Of spheres of existence is actual,
> Here the past and future
> Are conquered, and reconciled.[19]

Not to admit, therefore, to these four ends of Death, Judgment, Heaven, and Hell, the Catholic believer can be neither Catholic nor believing, because here is the central deposit from which all else is derived; here begins the vibrant and unending narrative of the Christian life, the long journey home to God. In order to function at even the most minimal level of Christian awareness, one has got to face the questions that, in Pascal's phrase, take us by the throat: How am I to die a good and holy Death? How am I to meet Judgment before God? How am I to avoid Hell? How am I to obtain Heaven?

When everything depends on how one squares off before these questions, and none are at liberty not to face each searing encounter, then the key element in the whole process becomes, in a word, hope. Without doubt, the theological virtue of hope is *the* defining experience when facing the End. In the confrontation with that which is uppermost in the Christian life (which includes all that could finally imperil that life, that is, the deadly risk we run of not attaining everlasting life, of life reduced to hopelessness), nothing is more necessary to understand, and so to draw upon, than the deepest possible reserves of hope.

[18] Eliot, *Four Quartets,* pp. 15–16.
[19] Ibid., p. 44.

If one speaks of life as a journey, and so as a road to be entered upon and traveled along, it is clear that it has three parts: life begins; it must end; and in between there exist passing moments (which, even as I write these words, fall haplessly away). The notion of eschatology, then, to reach for an exact definition here, is the study that seeks to throw as much light as possible on the End. Once again, the chief, operative virtue in piercing the mystery that presently surrounds the End is hope.

Life is a drama, the poets tell us, a struggle, fraught with immense eschatological tension. Surely this is the meaning, not often stressed these days, of membership in a Church Militant? Our lives are the stuff of titanic discords, of continual strife with the world, the flesh, and, yes, the devil. And the outcome of a man's effort athwart these forces will fix his fate for all eternity. Isn't this why hope must be theological? To begin with, like all mysteries rooted in God, hope orders and habituates one's life to participate more and more deeply in *his* life. Then there is the fact that God alone possesses the right and power to impart hope; no human construct gives rise to real hope. "The only genuine hope", says Gabriel Marcel, "is one directed toward something that does not depend on us."[20] And, finally, neither the existence of, nor the necessity for, supernatural hope can be deduced apart from Divine Revelation; only God can account for the deepest hungers of the human heart.

Immanuel Kant, having asked the question that he tells us is of supreme, compelling concern to man—namely, "What may I hope?"—immediately adds that of course only God can

---

[20] Quoted in Josef Pieper, *Hope and History* (San Francisco: Ignatius Press, 1994), p. 24.

answer it.[21] Why? Because it is he alone who has insinuated the hope of Heaven in our hearts. If God inscribes a purpose in human life, which purpose is meant to carry us beyond human life, that is, to Heaven, then it surely follows that only he can account for the hope and the Heaven. And while we have yet to find the object of this hope, stumbling blindly about a dark and broken world, we can see this much, that we are faced with the nagging presence of an absence, a continual haunting that fills us with longing. Certainly we have not found it amid the myriad of objects we do experience, none of which can ultimately satisfy. So hope tells us it may perhaps lie elsewhere. And like tiny children unwrapping a thousand tissued fripperies, suffering to repeat after each, "Is that all there is?" we hearken to the whispered importunities of One who answers, "No, there is more, much more, but it is not here."

It can only be God, then, for whom the restless human heart remains ever restless. The Elizabethan poet George Herbert put it superbly in a poem in which we observe God deploying that divine wit whereby we humans are drawn home to him (hence the title "The Pulley"):

> When God at first made man,
> Having a glass of blessings standing by,
> Let us (said He) pour on him all We can.
> Let the world's riches, which dispersed lie,
>   Contract into a span.
> So Strength first made a way;
> Then Beauty flowed; then Wisdom, Honor, Pleasure.

[21] Immanuel Kant, *Critique of Pure Reason,* trans. Norman Kemp Smith (New York: Macmillan, 1958), p. 635. "All the interests of my reason," he argues, "speculative as well as practical, combine in the three following questions: 1. What can I know? 2. What ought I to do? 3. What may I hope?"

When almost all was out, God made a stay,
Perceiving that alone, of all his treasure,
Rest in the bottom lay.
For if I should (said He)
Bestow this jewel also on my creature,
He would adore My gifts instead of Me,
And rest in Nature, not the God of Nature;
So both should losers be.
   Yet let him keep the rest,
But keep them with repining restlessness;
   Let him be rich and weary, that at least,
If goodness lead him not, yet weariness
   May toss him to My breast.[22]

Nearly three centuries after Herbert, the French poet Charles Péguy, who perished in the first weeks of the Great War, composed his unforgettable lyric on hope, "The Portal of the Mystery of the Second Virtue", in which God likewise speaks:

I AM, says God, Master of the Three Virtues.

Faith is a faithful wife.
Charity is an ardent mother.
But hope is a tiny girl.

I am, says God, Master of Virtues.

Faith is she who remains steadfast during centuries
   and centuries.
Charity is she who gives herself during centuries
   and centuries.
But my little hope is she
Who rises every morning.

[22] See *Images of Grace: 33 Christian Poems,* selected and introduced by Regis Martin (Steubenville, Ohio: Franciscan University Press, 1994), p. 3.

I am, says God, the Lord of Virtues.

Faith is she who remains tense during centuries
    and centuries.
Charity is she who unbends during centuries
    and centuries.
But my little hope
is she who every morning
wishes us good day.[23]

In the confession of faith drawn up some years ago by the German bishops, hope is described as "prototypically human",

[23] Charles Péguy, *God Speaks,* translated and introduced by Julian Green (New York: Pantheon, 1943), p. 93. The poem concludes most beautifully too:

> I am, says God, the Lord of virtues.
> Faith is the sanctuary lamp
> That burns forever.
> Charity is that big, beautiful log fire
> That you light in your hearth
> So that my children the poor may come and warm
>   themselves before it on winter evenings.
> And all around Faith, I see all my faithful
> Kneeling together in the same attitude, and with
>   one voice
> Uttering the same prayer.
> And around Charity, I see all my poor
> Sitting in a circle around that fire
> And holding out their palms to the heat of the
>   hearth.
> But my hope is the bloom, and the fruit, and the
>   leaf, and the limb,
> And the twig, and the shoot, and the seed, and
>   the bud.
> Hope is the shoot, and the bud of the bloom
>   Of eternity itself (pp. 102–3).

as that without which man cannot live.[24] In fact, in the synod that drafted the text, it bore the title "Our Hope", thus situating the whole dynamism of faith in the context of hope. What the German bishops sought was an understanding of hope as the sine qua non of the Christian life; the hard currency, as it were, to be used in negotiating our way home to God. Think of it, in view of Péguy's poem, as the human capacity, under the impetus of grace, to rise and greet God each day; and thus to get home in the end, on our last day. Hope is the virtue that most enables us to overcome the abyss separating time from eternity, man from God. Very different, therefore, from mere desire, which simply wishes that somehow things might work out. "Hope reaches deeper and goes farther. It is an expectation that the bleak monotony and burden of everyday life, the inequality and injustice in the world, the reality of evil and suffering will not have the last word, are not the ultimate reality."[25]

In short, hope persists in the conviction, nourished on faith, that reality is forever open to something—to Someone!—infinitely more. "Hope, like love," writes Josef Pieper, "is one of the very simple, primordial dispositions of the living person. In hope, man reaches 'with restless heart', with confidence and patient expectation, toward the *bonun arduum futurum,* toward the arduous 'not yet' of fulfillment, whether natural or supernatural."[26]

This persisting tendency was nicely caught in a *New Yorker* cartoon of some years back. Two prisoners are huddled in a doorless, windowless dungeon, the walls stretching straight up for fifty feet. Escape is clearly impossible. Yet one prisoner is

---

[24] *The Church's Confession of Faith,* p. 327.
[25] Ibid.
[26] Josef Pieper, *On Hope* (San Francisco: Ignatius Press, 1986), p. 27.

saying to the other, "Now here's my plan." At the very core of man's being, it would appear, there is that oddly indomitable impulse for more, an irrepressibility of soul unsatisfied with circumstance or self, hoping thereby to make a more perfect future of each. Like God's "tiny girl . . . who rises every morning", hope seeks to render each day its due allotment of justice and praise. In this sense man is his own future. Tomorrow enters decisively into today in order to give imaginative shape to the texture of all that we think or know or feel—indeed, who we are. Our lives are meant to become, to use the image of the poet John Keats, a vale of soul making.

Real hope, the stuff that endures in the teeth of every adversity, is neither cheap grace, costing God nothing to confer (we scarcely can imagine the price paid in order for us to spend such prodigal amounts),[27] nor the foolish optimism of those who, in love with Professor Coue's creed, actually believe everything in every way is getting better and better every day (passing acquaintance with the law of entropy, to say nothing of a newspaper, should put that nonsense to rest). No, real hope is hard, the provenance of which can only be theological, which means a hope ever trained on God, who we trustfully expect will provide all that he has promised. In other words, despite every indication that, humanly speaking, his situation

---

[27] "Many people think that it is simply up to them to reconcile themselves with God, and that many do not need such reconciliation at all. . . . They have no conception of the flames necessary to burn up all the refuse that is within man; they have no idea that these flames burn white hot in the Cross of Jesus. There is a cry that penetrates all the cool pharisaism of our alleged religiosity: 'My God, my God, why have you forsaken me?' In the darkest night of the soul, while every fiber of his body is in pain, and he experiences extreme thirst for God, for lost love, he atones for our comfortable indifference." Hans Urs von Balthasar, *You Crown the Year with Your Goodness: Radio Sermons* (San Francisco: Ignatius Press, 1989), p. 79.

is hopeless—a disaster, a washout—the man possessed of hope soldiers on, fully confident that God can somehow retrieve matters, that they need not remain forever steeped in tragic futility. In hope man always transcends the empirically given situation. The *Catechism of the Catholic Church* puts it this way: "Hope is the confident expectation of divine blessing and the beatific vision of God." It is also, the text continues, "the fear", which can be a most healthy and holy thing, "of offending God's love and of incurring punishment".[28] To recall the Act of Contrition, which for centuries countless penitents have repeated, one is sorry for sin not only because of the everlasting ruin that awaits the unrepentant but "most of all because Thou art all good and deserving of all my love".

Hope is accordingly the virtue most peculiar to man on the way, in transit, in parentheses between time and eternity, which Pieper rightly traces back to "the innermost structure of created nature" itself, the inherent "not yet" of all finite being. "The 'way' of *homo viator*," he writes, "of man 'on the way', is not a directionless back-and-forth between being and nothingness; it leads toward being and away from nothingness; it leads to realization, not to annihilation, although this realization is 'not yet' fulfilled and the fall into nothingness is 'not yet' impossible."[29]

Hope thus is the virtue by which man best understands his creaturely status, the essential tension in which he exists, poised between being and nothingness, Heaven and Hell. And it is given to man to possess in order precisely to sustain him in his pilgrim state and thus to thwart the two deadliest of tempta-

---

[28] *Catechism of the Catholic Church* (Rome: Libreria Editrice Vaticana, 1994), no. 2090, p. 507. Hereafter cited as CCC.

[29] Pieper, *On Hope*, p. 20.

tions that threaten to overthrow the citadel of his hope, that of despair, which refuses any longer to hope, or presumption, which imagines that one can obtain fulfillment without it. For man to countenance either is to sin against the First Commandment, which obliges us to worship and serve God alone.

On whom, then, is our hope finally anchored? The answer is plain: Jesus the Christ, who, in the prayer that he gave us, the only prayer our Blessed Lord explicitly taught, grounds the whole eschatological enterprise of Christian hope: hope rooted in the Father, through the Son, from whom all good things come, including most especially this gift of salvation poured out upon the world. The Our Father, the *Catechism* tells us, "is the proper prayer of the 'end-time,' the time of salvation that began with the outpouring of the Holy Spirit and will be fulfilled with the Lord's return".[30] It is especially in the Eucharistic Sacrifice, which provides the most intimate and privileged sacramental foretaste of the heavenly banquet to come, that these eschatological vibrations are most resonantly felt, the petitionary inflections most clearly shown. "From this unshakable faith springs forth the hope that sustains each of the seven petitions, which express the groanings of the present age, this time of patience and expectation during which 'it does not yet appear what we shall be.' The Eucharist and the Lord's Prayer look eagerly for the Lord's return, 'until he comes.' "[31]

In the Scriptures we confront the following datum of faith; it is one whose relevance to eschatology, the Last Things, cannot be overstated. It is that Christ, before his miraculous ascent to the Father and thus the completion of the circuit

---

[30] CCC, 2771.
[31] CCC, 2772.

begun thirty-three years before with the descent into the human condition, basically made two promises to his apostles, those first leaders of the nascent Christian community fashioned from his pierced body on the Cross. These were: "I go and prepare a place for you . . . that where I am you may be also."[32] And: "I shall not leave you orphans."[33] Two promises, one for eternity, the other for time, the condition of this contingent world. Two sublime and mysterious gifts, committed to those whom he loved to the last: the gift of everlasting life and the capacity to endure even this life (this latter gift pursuant, as always, to that other, more glorious life across the threshold of death). Both gifts locked in the treasury of the Holy Church, the Bride of Christ, whose keys unlock the secrets of the Kingdom of Heaven.

Before taking leave of his disciples, then, Christ is at great pains to assure them that he is not simply tossing their lives and futures to the four winds. Instead, he tells them, they and the Church, and all her members to the end of time, shall be guided and shaped across the great and fearful sea of history by a very special wind, namely, the breath of God's own Spirit, who will infallibly confer both comfort and counsel upon this Pilgrim People, Christ's Mystical Body. The Lord says, "I am with you always, until the end of the world."[34] The form this being-with-you takes is of course the Third Person of the Trinity, the very One who from all eternity spirates the love of Father and Son. He is God's presence within us, in our

[32] See Jn 14:3.
[33] Jn 14:18.
[34] Mt 28:19.

innermost being, even as he remains effortlessly transcendent to us.[35]

This guarantee is first made at the Last Supper and subsequently given breathtaking expression in the fourteenth chapter of Saint John's Gospel. The loftiest charter of eschatological hope we have, it strikes the necessary note of continuity between the two promises and so in a single stroke resolves the basic tension between *already* and *not yet*. (Yes, salvation has come; but, no, the fullness thereof still awaits the End.) In its *Letter on Certain Questions Concerning Eschatology*, issued in 1979 by the Vatican's Sacred Congregation for the Doctrine of the Faith, the Church precisely reminds us of this fact, stressing what it calls "the fundamental continuity, thanks to the power of the Holy Spirit, between our present life in Christ and the future life".[36]

More recently, of course, Pope John Paul II, in *Crossing the Threshold of Hope*, has made the same point. Speaking of the truth that the Gospel teaches us about God, he says that this truth "requires a certain *change in focus with regard to eschatology*. First of all, eschatology is not what will take place in the future, something happening only after earthly life is finished. *Eschatology has already begun with the coming of Christ*. The

[35] "This 'Spirit' is not simply identical either with the Father or the Son, nor yet a third thing erected between God and us; it is the mode in which God gives himself to us, in which he enters into us, so that he is *in* man, yet in the midst of this 'indwelling' is infinitely *above* him." Joseph Ratzinger, *Introduction to Christianity* (San Francisco: Ignatius Press, 1990), p. 115.

[36] Sacred Congregation for the Doctrine of the Faith, *Letter on Certain Questions Concerning Eschatology* (Boston: Daughters of St. Paul, 1979), p. 8.

ultimate eschatological event was His redemptive Death and His Resurrection. This is the beginning of 'a new heaven and a new earth' (cf. Rev 21:1)."[37]

Faith, in other words, may now find itself bathed in overwhelming eschatological light. And not only faith. Theology, too, says Hans Urs von Balthasar, "must be dominated by the *eschata,* become 'eschatologized', for now the world, man, and history realize their true nature only when subjected to God's transforming action".[38] Or, to quote the uncompromising language of the early Barth: "A Christianity that is not wholly, entirely and absolutely eschatology has wholly, entirely and absolutely nothing to do with Christ."[39]

Eschatology is thus a message of unsurpassed joy. The destiny of the world was definitively determined the moment Christ burst the bonds of death. Heaven is ours. Amid the flux of the temporal, the muck and muddle of mere ambiguity, the

[37] John Paul II, *Crossing the Threshold of Hope,* edited by Vittorio Messori (New York: Knopf, 1994), pp. 184–85.

[38] Hans Urs von Balthasar, "Some Points of Eschatology", in *Explorations in Theology: The Word Made Flesh* (San Francisco: Ignatius Press, 1989), p. 259.

[39] Quoted by Joseph Ratzinger, *Principles of Catholic Theology* (San Francisco: Ignatius Press, 1987), p. 176. "His method", notes Balthasar in his seminal study of Barth, "is to bring everything to the point of highest intensity: where God and man intersect in Jesus Christ. . . . We could describe this thought as a kind of hourglass, where the two contiguous vessels (God and creature) meet only at the narrow passage through the center: where they both encounter each other in Jesus Christ. The purpose of the image is to show that there is no other point of contact between the two chambers of the glass. And just as the sand flows only from top to bottom, so too God's revelation is one-sided, flowing from his gracious decision alone. But of course the sand flows down into the other chamber so that the sand there can really *increase.* In other words, there *is* a countermovement in the other chamber, but only because of the first movement, the initiative of the first chamber." *The Theology of Karl Barth* (San Francisco: Ignatius Press, 1992), p. 197.

Last Things are at work. Nothing can separate us from the love of God save our own perverse refusal to be loved. The light of Heaven shines wherever a flame, however flickering, burns with the hard, gemlike flame of Christ. No hope will suffer final disillusion.[40]

And so the ground of man belongs in a certain sense, and at every turn in the road, to the goal of being human. I come from God, I go to God, and all the moments in between belong to God. The poet Hopkins has put it in as fine a lyric of eschatological hope as can be found in the language:

> Thee, God, I come from, to thee go,
> All day long I like fountain flow
> From thy hand out, swayed about
> Mote-like in thy mighty glow.[41]

---

[40] In his book on Barth, the theme of "dynamic eschatology" is described, which Barth gave striking expression to in his *Epistle to the Romans*. It is, says Balthasar, "the irreversible movement from a fatally doomed temporal order to a new living order filled with the life of God, the restoration (*apokatastasis*) of the original ideal creation in God. This 'movement' of a doomed world, which still knows its true origin but cannot get back to it on its own, is due solely to God's graciousness in Christ. In Christ, God has implanted life in the whole of the cosmos; this life is a seed that will dynamically sprout and spread irresistibly until everything is transformed back into its original splendor. This will not take place in plain view but will work itself out eschatologically" (*Theology of Karl Barth,* p. 64). Nevertheless, Balthasar is not here endorsing the view, which Barth himself gave evidence of holding from time to time, that in the end one could expect all things to be reconciled to God, yes, even creatures the obduracy of whose evil choices have taken them to Hell. Such an understanding of *apokatastasis* stands formally condemned by the Church, and Balthasar does not, for that reason, wish to associate himself with it, not even as a working hypothesis, which was the ground on which Origen ventured his defense.

[41] *Poems of Gerard Manley Hopkins,* 3d ed. (New York and London: Oxford University Press, 1948), no. 116, p. 167.

How, in very practical terms, could it be otherwise? If God is love, and love therefore the law of the Kingdom, the coin of the heavenly realm, then the practice of it in the body of this world will surely constitute the measure of our share in future glory. Admission to the place where Christ has gone will finally turn on the extent to which we have lived, not as orphans bent on brutalizing one another but as brothers and sisters united in a common love of Christ. As Saint John of the Cross reminds us, "At the evening of life, we shall be judged on our love."[42]

So it is no small matter that the Vatican, in its CDF report, is here addressing. The profound and intimate connection between the way we conduct our moral lives in this world and the Judgment awaiting us in the next is an unalterable rule of faith. How can Heaven exist for those who have made a Hell on earth? And, conversely, how does one rightly weigh the worth of a man's charity in this world if not by the joy and beatitude awaiting him in the next? What other recompense is there to compensate him for a life of rectitude? The Pope, incidentally, in lamenting a certain evanescence of eschatological awareness among Christians

---

[42] Cited in CCC, 1022. The concluding stanzas of the Hopkins poem quoted above precisely give evidence of this primacy of love to be shown to others:

> I have life before me still
> And thy purpose to fulfil;
> Yea a debt to pay thee yet:
> Help me, sir, and so I will.

> But thou bidst, and just thou art,
> Me shew mercy from my heart
> Towards my brother, every other
> Man my mate and counterpart.

(eschatology, he says, "to a certain degree . . . has become irrelevant to contemporary man"), nevertheless argues that *"faith in God, as Supreme Justice,* has not become irrelevant to man; the expectation remains that there is Someone who, in the end, will be able to speak the truth about the good and evil which man does, Someone able to reward the good and punish the bad."[43]

However, there is this perduring note of discontinuity to be made also, which consists of a deep, lasting disharmony at the heart of every redeemed actuality. Yes, we believe grace builds on nature; yet at the same time grace infinitely exceeds nature. The two orders are manifestly disjoined even as they come together in the life of man. "Out of all bodies and minds," writes Pascal, "we could not extract one impulse of true charity. It is impossible, and of a different, supernatural order."[44] The coin of the true realm, which is charity, is not minted by men and can only fall, gratuitously, from above, where God dwells in inaccessible light. Here is how the Congregation for the Doctrine of the Faith has put it: "Christians . . . must be clearly aware of the radical break between the present life and the future one, due to the fact that the economy of faith will be replaced by the economy of fullness of life; we shall be with Christ and 'we shall see God' (cf. 1 Jn 3:2), and it is in these

---

43 John Paul II, *Crossing the Threshold of Hope,* pp. 183–84.

44 Pascal, *Pensées,* no. 308, pp. 123–25. Pascal is here making the point that among the orders of body, mind, and soul, the latter being the origin of the life of charity, there is such a note of discontinuity that no music can result that harmonizes one with another, in the absence, that is, of any higher intervention. In other words, the fulfillment of carnal life does not, of itself, provide a bridge across which lies the perfection of intellect. Still less will the combination of the two produce the grace note of love. "All bodies together and all minds together and all their products are not worth the least impulse of charity. This is of an infinitely superior order."

promises and marvelous mysteries that our hope essentially consists."[45]

Once again, the end becomes the beginning. As Father Ladislaus Boros states, "Life was designed by God for Heaven. Man is to be comprehended in his fullness, that is, from Heaven's viewpoint . . . life is a turning towards Heaven. Life is not yet here. Real life merely approaches us."[46] A very moving and beautiful confirmation of this truth occurs in the film version of the Pope's play *The Jeweler's Shop*. A young Polish priest comes to the home of the grieving widow whose husband has just died, fighting to resist the Nazi takeover of their country. What does one say at such a moment? He tells her, very simply, the truth, which is that her husband is "more alive now" than ever he might have been in the flesh. She accepts this because she believes, because she has hope.

But who can sustain this claim? How are the two orders of earth and Heaven to be held together? (Indeed, as regards a whole series of vexed issues—for example, nature and grace, time and eternity, history and Heaven, God and man—what is it that causes any of these to cohere, to achieve an integrity of expression, a congruity of life?) Clearly the cement, the magic glue connecting these and countless other disparate elements we encounter, is Christ. He alone is the mediating force and principle, and, to be sure, he is not any force or principle, he is no abstraction, but a Person, the Word of the Father whose eternal utterance now reaches into the silence of all that is not Father, in order to give it speech, to uphold the world by the sheer weight of his Word. We do not exist save as a word

---

45 *Letter on Certain Questions of Eschatology*, p. 8.
46 Ladislaus Boros, S.J., "The New Heaven and the New Earth", *Readings in Christian Eschatology* (Derby, N.Y.: Society of St. Paul, 1966), p. 22.

spoken by Another, by God the eternal Word. "For Christ plays in ten thousand places", as Hopkins tells us,

> Lovely in limbs, and lovely in eyes not his
> To the Father through the features of men's faces.[47]

The poet Rilke has likewise caught the idea, the master intuition, and brings it exquisitely to life, to art. This is from the final stanza of his poem "Autumn":

> We all are falling. This hand falls.
> And look at others: it is in them all.
> And yet there is one who holds this falling
> Endlessly gently in His hands.[48]

"All the way to Heaven is Heaven, because Christ is the Way." That is how Saint Catherine of Siena would put it, no doubt instructed to say so by Christ himself, who often appeared to her, indeed, teaching her — this future Doctor of the Roman Catholic Church — how to read. "Nothing that you do or can do", he once told her, "pleases me as much as when you believe that I love you." Certainly his having created us amounts to God's first down payment on that investment of love. Christ, then, is the single overarching Presence in our lives, in the life of the cosmos, and on the strength of that Presence we take comfort, pleasure even, in the fact that we are not alone, not entirely poor despite our creaturely status. We know, as any medieval exegete can tell us, that the world we live in is a book, an endlessly rich and evocative text, which constantly speaks to us with humility and joy. Bespeaking its own emptiness, yes, but always and everywhere the presence of Another, God,

---

47 Hopkins, *Poems,* no. 57, p. 95.
48 Translations from *The Poetry of Rainer Maria Rilke,* by M. D. Herter Norton (New York: Norton, 1938), p. 75.

its Creator and Redeemer. "Dante speaks to us of God," Eric Gill used to say, "but so do the daisies, the dew drops, and the dung." Nature is a parable.

Indeed, we may all be the most metaphysically miserable of beings—a myriad examples of wretched nothingness, of cosmic impoverishment—but Someone has brought us freely into being and evidently delights to hold and sustain all that blessed nothingness in being. As Augustine once put it in describing the being of God, and the implication to be fleshed out from that primal fact (to wit, the sheer convertibility of being with the other transcendentals): "Because He is good, we are, and inasmuch as He is, we are good." The world and all who dwell therein are thus mysteriously formed in the image of God. And so movement between God and ourselves is possible. God desires, however, the perfection of that image in order to confer the likeness of divine sonship. Accordingly, he sends our roots rain in the form of that grace that is the nurture of our lives. In Christ, therefore, nature takes on grace, is gathered onto the plane of glory. And Old Testament figure becomes New Testament fulfillment. He alone enables us to repair the rent in our nature, to heal the world's body, in short, to overcome the distance between "already" and "not yet". As von Balthasar describes it in his groundbreaking essay on eschatology, "the distinction between time of promise and time of fulfillment, in fact between the three times of mere promise (the Old Testament), of fulfilled promise along with fulfillment promised (the Church of the New Testament), and complete fulfillment (eschatology)",[49] is a distinction precisely pointing to Christ. Only he can reach down deeply and efficaciously enough into the marrow of this world, amid its wounded and shattered state, to perform the neces-

---

[49] Balthasar, "Some Points of Eschatology", in *Explorations in Theology: The Word Made Flesh*, pp. 271–72.

sary transmutative surgery to effect the world's cure. "Across my foundering deck", writes Hopkins, in surely his most triumphant lyric mode, to wit, his extraordinary poem, "That Nature Is a Heraclitean Fire and of the Comfort of the Resurrection",

> ... shone
> A beacon, an eternal beam. Flesh fade, and mortal
>   trash
> Fall to the residuary worm; a world's wildfire,
> leave but ash:
>   In a flash, at a trumpet crash,
> I am all at once what Christ is, since he was
>   what I am, and
> This Jack, joke, poor potsherd, patch,
>   matchwood, immortal diamond
>   Is immortal diamond.[50]

Balthasar's thesis anticipates one of the profound themes of *Lumen Gentium*, particularly chapter 7, "The Eschatological Nature of the Pilgrim Church and Her Union with the Heavenly Church", which shows how the Church's promised consummation in glory is not only a gift for the far side of paradise but one whose mysterious unfolding may be seen even in this life. Why? Because, once more, Christ, the whole meaning of whose life and mission is to be "lifted up from the earth", will necessarily draw all men to himself.[51] Thus the world is destined to be wedded to the Word, a mysterious union that Christ himself mediates in that space we call the Church.[52]

---

[50] Hopkins, *Poems*, no. 72, p. 112.

[51] Jn 12:32.

[52] "Therefore, the promised restoration which we are awaiting has already begun in Christ, is carried forward in the mission of the Holy Spirit, and through Him continues in the Church", *Lumen Gentium*, no. 48.

"The final age of the world has already come upon us (cf. 1 Cor. 10:11). The renovation of the world has been irrevocably decreed and in this age is already anticipated in some real way."[53]

Pieper, in a very telling passage from his book *On Hope,* which sounds the tocsin of Christ as "the actual fulfillment of our hope" (again, this note of both/and), goes on to cite a couple of passages from Saint Augustine, which brilliantly testify to his theme. In the first text Augustine interprets the Pauline verse from Romans "In hope were we saved" (8:24) as follows: "But Paul did not say, 'we shall be saved', but 'we have already been saved'; yet not in fact [*re*], but in hope; he says, 'in hope were we saved'. This hope we have in Christ, for in him is fulfilled all that we hope for by his promise." And in the second text Augustine once again anchors hope to Christ: "As yet we do not see that for which we hope. But we are the body of that Head in whom that for which we hope is brought to fulfillment."[54]

Of such crucial and transcendent importance is this linkage to Christ that for anyone not to be in Christ is in effect to be without hope. Apart from Christ, who is our hope, we are simply and entirely bereft. Alternatively, of course, to the degree one is in Christ, steeped in the sacramental life of the Church in which, among other benefactions, the blessings of hope are dispensed, to that very extent one possesses hope, of which there is literally no limit in this or the next world. One thinks here of course of Saint Thérèse of Lisieux, the sheer limitlessness of whose hope in God has become the distinctive mark, the very signature of her sanctity. "I believe", she says, referring to God and his saints, "that they are waiting to see

53 Ibid.
54 Pieper, *On Hope,* p. 35.

how far I will go in my trust, but not in vain was my heart
pierced by that saying of Job's: 'Even if you kill me, I will have
hope in you.' Believe in the truth of what I now say: we can
never have too much trust in our dear God, who is so powerful
and so merciful. One receives as much from him as one hopes
for." And in serene expectation of the heavenly mission she
longs to receive, Thérèse declares, "All of my expectations will
be more than richly fulfilled; indeed the Lord will do something wondrous for me that will infinitely exceed even my
boundless wishes."[55]

Nevertheless, leaving aside the example of the Little Flower,
so singularly unsurpassed was the quality of *her* Christian
hope, one wonders how many of her coreligionists these days
are prepared to evince as lively an awareness and ardor for the
"always more" aspect of God's mercy. How hungry indeed are
we for hope? "If your justice feels inclined to discharge itself"—so
Thérèse addresses her Lord—"that *which, after all, extends only
over the earth,* how much more, then, does your merciful love
yearn to *inflame* souls, because your mercy, after all, *ascends
all the way up to heaven*" (cf. Ps 36:6).[56] What a staggering
statement! The mind reels before the apparent overmastery of
divine justice by mercy. But, really, how many of us are even
interested? Alas, how few the number of Christians who con-
tinue even to profess belief that Christ, the Son of God, by his
return to the Father has in fact gone to prepare a place for us.
Saint Augustine, in a wonderful catechesis intended for aspir-
ing Christians of his own time, loosed a thunderbolt for our
own, which seems almost to despair of the Good News. Faith,
he tells the catechumens of the fifth century, is the presupposi-

[55] Quoted in Hans Urs von Balthasar, *Dare We Hope "That All Men
Be Saved"?* (San Francisco: Ignatius Press, 1988), p. 103, see pp. 102–5.
[56] Ibid., p. 102.

tion for whatever understanding is to follow. "Christ ascended into Heaven. Believe! He sits at the right hand of the Father. Believe! . . . He is there! Do not let your heart say, 'What is he doing?' Do not ask what we are not permitted to find out! He is there! That is enough for you! He is in bliss, and it is from the bliss that is called 'the right hand of the Father' that the name of this bliss is derived: 'the right hand of the Father'."[57]

From this event of incomparable bliss, a glorious cornucopia of joy and delight endlessly awaits those who love God. As Balthasar puts it, "his 'return' to the Father is the *creation of the dimension* into which, by the free grace of God, man and the cosmos begin to be transformed".[58] In other words, Jesus Christ by the event of his Resurrection and ascension is in fact the real beginning of Heaven. Indeed, it is the final and dramatic conjunction of the two orders, nature and grace, the two beings, man and God; an event that holds out to all mankind the real possibility of everlasting life. Love is finally stronger than death because God, who is Love, is risen from the dead. This, then, is the beginning of eschatological life, of the definitive breach of that frontier imposed by sin and death. Both my own longings for immortality, and those of other men, may now freely converge upon Christ, who is Alpha and Omega, beginning and end of history. But again, how many of us are inclined to live on so exalted a level of transformation? Perhaps eternal bliss is not nearly banal enough for our earthbound appetites. Maybe God overdid the compliment he paid us when, as Augustine put it in the aftermath of his conversion,

<hr />

57 *Sermo ad Catechumenos* IV, 11, quoted in Christoph Schönborn, *From Death to Life: The Christian Journey* (San Francisco: Ignatius Press, 1995), p. 23.

58 Balthasar, "Some Points of Eschatology", in *Explorations in Theology: The Word Made Flesh*, p. 262.

"You had pierced our hearts with the arrows of your love, and we carried your words with us as though they were staked to our living bodies."[59] Maybe mankind would rather he have left us alone, unpierced by the lance of Divine Love.

But if not, then it becomes at once terrifyingly clear that it is God himself who *is* the Last Thing ever to be remembered. "Gained, he is heaven; lost, he is Hell; examining, he is judgment, purifying, he is purgatory. He it is to whom finite being dies, and through whom it rises to him, in him. This he is, however, as he presents himself to the world, that is, in his Son, *Jesus Christ,* who is the revelation of God and, therefore, the whole essence of the last things. In this way," concludes Balthasar, "eschatology is, almost more even than any other *locus theologicus,* entirely a doctrine of *salvation.* "[60]

To what extent are convictions like these still operative in the lives of Christian men and women? Do we not live, for the most part, in the aftermath of the disappearance and death of God, of the extinction therefore of all hope? "Holy Saturday: the day God was buried; isn't this remarkably true of our day, today? Is not our century starting to be one long Holy Saturday, the day God was absent . . . ?" So wrote Joseph Ratzinger in an Easter meditation for 1969.[61] In it he wonders aloud if the Church and the faith she represents have not come to "resemble a little boat which is about to sink, which is battling futilely against the waves and the wind, and all the time God is absent?" A profound sorrow steals over the soul, seeming to divest it of hope for God, for the life to come. "An anguish comes, the real type of anguish born in the depths of our

---

[59] See his *Confessions,* bk. IX, chap. 2.

[60] Balthasar, "Some Points of Eschatology", in *Explorations in Theology: The Word Made Flesh,* pp. 260–61.

[61] "The Anguish of an Absence", reproduced by *30 Days,* no. 3, 1994.

solitudes, that cannot be cast out by reason but only by the presence of a person who loves us." And, alas, he is gone because by our forgetfulness we have allowed his presence to evanesce from our lives.[62]

Here then is the modern, secularist temptation with which the Church's doctrine of the Last Things must do battle. The task, which is the same in this and every age, is to awaken the world to God, to the music of the heavenly spheres, the eternal poetry of the transcendent, whence cometh the Word into the world whereby God's enfleshment brings man salvation. The Church's mission is to lead the world home to God. ("But our homeland is in Heaven," declares Paul, "whence we also await the savior, Our Lord Jesus Christ.")[63] The Church is obliged, as always, to direct our minds and wills across the threshold of hope; for we cannot be happy unless we feed on hope, on the hope of Heaven. "Seek the things that are above," Paul enjoins us, "where Christ is, seated at the right hand of God. Strive to attain what is above, not what is on earth".[64]

And, finally, who but God himself can fill the human heart, slaking this deepest thirst of all, that of unending joy? C. S. Lewis has noted how "the faint, far-off results of those energies which God's creative rapture implanted in matter when He made the worlds are what we now call physical pleasures; and even thus filtered, they are too much for our present management. What would it be", he asks, "to taste at the fountainhead that stream of which even these lower reaches prove so intoxicating? Yet that, I believe, is what lies before us. The

[62] For a further and more extensive treatment of this theme, which is so painfully eloquent of our time, see my book *The Suffering of Love: Christ's Descent into the Hell of Human Hopelessness* (Petersham, Mass.: St. Bede's Press, 1995).

[63] Phil 3:20.

[64] Col 3:1–2.

whole man is to drink joy from the fountain of joy. As St. Augustine said, the rapture of the saved soul will 'flow over' into the glorified body. In the light of our present special-ised and depraved appetites, we cannot imagine this *torrens voluptatis.*"[65]

Nor are we advised to try. Yet, faced with so absolutely enrapturing a prospect, which hope imparts, why not give the pursuit of it a try? Let the celestial chips fall where they may. "And so it is appointed that men die once, and then comes Judgment."[66] After which, we have it on faith, there looms, breathtakingly, an eternity of gain or loss, Heaven or Hell, to await those whom God first graciously brought into being. We are all free moral agents, and so, given the trajectory of our lives, we take ourselves, from beginning to end, to one or the other possibility. But at the very last, as the Pope reminds us, it is Love himself to whom we present ourselves. *"Before all else, it is Love that judges.* God, who is Love, judges through love."[67] It is he whom we encounter in the End, the Same who made us in the beginning, the One on whom we hope for strength and support along the way.

[65] C. S. Lewis, *The Weight of Glory and Other Addresses* (Grand Rapids, Mich.: Eerdmans, 1977), p. 14.

[66] Heb 9:27.

[67] *Crossing the Threshold of Hope,* p. 187.

Death

A number of years ago, an unknown English author and Catholic convert by the name of Muriel Spark (she has since become more widely known) wrote a very startling and unusual novel of macabre and prophetic humor called *Memento Mori*.[1] An unsparing, utterly unsentimental account of Death, the book achieved immediate and wide critical acclaim. Writers of long-established reputation such as Graham Greene and Evelyn Waugh did not hesitate to pronounce it brilliant and ingenious, the work of a mature, strikingly original talent. Indeed, it succeeded with weapons of considerable elegance and wit in rending a good deal of the oppressive silence then surrounding the subject of Death, what the critic V. S. Pritchett called, in an admiring review of the book, "the great suppressed and censored subject of contemporary society".

Dame Lettie Colston, on whom the story opens, is writing a letter when her telephone rings and she hears a voice speaking to her. "Remember", it says, "you must die." It is the ninth time the mysterious caller has telephoned to remind her. Meanwhile, phones are ringing out across the city, notifying members of Dame Lettie's set of their inevitable end. And

[1] See Muriel Spark, *Memento Mori* (reprint, New York: Time-Life Books, 1964). (Originally published by J. B. Lippincott, 1958.)

though it is Death himself calling, few are thankful enough for the salutary summons. Instead they are thrown into sudden panic and consternation, wave upon wave of senile annoyance sweeping over them.

In due course, an investigation is begun, led by retired Inspector Mortimer, another member of the set (he is in his seventies), whom Death, strangely, has not called; it won't matter when he does, a lifetime's remembrance of death having kept Mortimer serene and alert. A meeting is quickly arranged, the victims arriving somewhat shaken in nerve and body. Various accounts of the outrage are heard, Mortimer giving the official version, which is one of complete bafflement. Despite, he says, "every method of detection known to criminology and science", the police are unable to trace the calls. Nevertheless, notes Mortimer, "there is one factor constant in all your reports. The words, 'Remember you must die.' It is, you know, an excellent thing to remember, for it is nothing more than the truth. To remember one's death is, in short, a way of life."

Earlier Mortimer had mused, much to Dame Lettie's annoyance (she thinks of death as an unwarranted and insolent affront to her dignity and will spare no effort to enlist Scotland Yard in tracking it down), "If I had my life over again I should form the habit of nightly composing myself to thoughts of death ... no other practice so intensifies life. Death, when it approaches, ought not to take one by surprise. It should be part of the full expectancy of life."

Every tale, I suppose, must have its truth, and Mortimer is not the only one to tell it. My favorite is Granny Taylor, who quite succeeded in getting her dying done every day. "A good death", she said, "doesn't reside in the dignity of bearing but in the disposition of the soul." Her own is movingly revealed at the very close of this exceptionally fine novel: "Jean Taylor lingered for a time, employing her pain to magnify the Lord, and meditating sometimes confidingly upon Death, the first of the Four Last Things to be ever remembered."

Not everyone faced with Death's sudden inexorability will prove as piously inclined as Granny Taylor. There are those who simply cannot bring themselves to the sticking point, who knowing death must soon unhinge the frail paneling of their lives nevertheless persist in refusing to face the summons. Like the fellow in the film *On Borrowed Time* (delightfully portrayed by Lionel Barrymore) who contrives to outwit Death, and like the English folktale on which it is based, who even succeeds for a time in keeping the Old Guy at bay, many of us will not go quietly into that good night. Instead, taking the advice of Welsh poet Dylan Thomas, we rage, some of us pretty mightily, against the dying of the light.[2] Or we are like the character Claudio in Shakespeare's *Measure for Measure,* whose initial and resolute impulse to forfeit life in order to save a beloved sister endears us to him ("If I must die," he bravely announces, "I will encounter darkness as a bride, / And hug it in mine arms"). But then the thought of death—the bloody prospect of actually having to do it!—so unnerves the poor man that he ends by asking his sister to forfeit her virtue for him! It is a speech fraught with the horror many associate with Death:

[2] See Thomas' poem "Do Not Go Gentle into That Good Night", movingly addressed to his dying father, whom he exhorts in his old age to "burn and rave at close of day". The concluding lines are particularly poignant:

> And you, my father, there on the sad height,
> Curse, bless, me now with your fierce tears,
>   I pray.
> Do not go gentle into that good night.
> Rage, rage against the dying of the light.

Ay, but to die, and go we know not where,
To lie in cold obstruction and to rot,
This sensible warm motion to become
A kneaded clod; and the delighted spirit
To bathe in fiery floods, or to reside
In thrilling region of thick-ribbed ice;
To be imprisoned in the viewless winds,
And blown with restless violence round about
The pendant world; or to be worse than worst
Of those that lawless and incertain thought
Imagine howling—'tis too horrible!
The weariest and most loathed worldly life
That age, ache, penury, and imprisonment
Can lay on nature is a paradise
To what we fear of death.[3]

Alas, even for us, we privileged recipients of four hundred years of progress since William Shakespeare, the sense of death, our death, remains so abhorrent a prospect that anything, yes,

---

[3] Act III, sc. 1, ll. 118–32. Shakespeare here pulls out all the stops of Elizabethan horror in the face of Death. Indeed, its sense of mounting doom and despair seems well nigh medieval. See J. Huizinga's classic study, *The Waning of the Middle Ages,* first published in 1924, whole sections of which seem uncannily reminiscent of the Elizabethan soul. Noting, for example, the late fourteenth-century tendency to evoke "all the horrors of decomposition", especially in pictorial art, which soon percolated from high ecclesiastical to low popular literature, he writes: "Until far into the sixteenth century, tombs are adorned with hideous images of a naked corpse with clenched hands and rigid feet, gaping mouth and bowels crawling with worms. The imagination of those times relished these horrors, without ever looking one stage further, to see how corruption perishes in its turn, and flowers grow where it lay" ([Garden City, N.Y.: Doubleday, 1954], p. 140). Amid the imagery of such mortal coils not a few of Shakespeare's characters are caught. So much for the myth of Renaissance man set free from morbid preoccupations with Death!

even penury and prison, seem positively paradisal compared to
the terrors that the thought of it awakens. And so we try not to
think of death, creating an unreal world wrapped in plastic
and cellophane to seal away the unpleasantness. We dismiss the
apprehension as atavistic, a species of benightedness that among
the many blessings of modern science we've managed to banish
from our workaday lives. Who, for example, any longer dies at
home, encircled by the love of those closest to him, including
his own children?

No, the practice nowadays is to isolate the patient in hospitals,
surrounded by machinery and technicians, neither of which
are particularly disposed to humanize the event. Yet we must
all die, some sooner than others to be sure, but all scheduled to
leave the theater at some point in the play. "The houses are all
gone under the sea", writes T. S. Eliot. "The dancers are all
gone under the hill."

> O dark dark dark. They all go into the dark,
> The vacant interstellar spaces, the vacant into the vacant,
> The captains, merchant bankers, eminent men of letters,
> The generous patrons of art, the statesmen and the rulers,
> Distinguished civil servants, chairmen of many committees,
> Industrial lords and petty contractors, all go into the dark,
> And dark the Sun and Moon, and the Almanach de Gotha
> And the Stock Exchange Gazette, the Directory of Directors,
> And cold the sense and lost the motive of action.
> And we all go with them, into the silent funeral,
> Nobody's funeral, for there is no one to bury.[4]

The point is, we must all go with them, into the same silent
funeral, consigned to a common grave of forgetfulness. "I said

4 From T. S. Eliot's *Four Quartets,* the third movement of "East
Coker" (New York: Harcourt, Brace and World, 1943).

to my soul, be still, and let the dark come upon you / Which shall be the darkness of God." For all the vaunted machinery of modern medicine, the cult of idolatrous youth, the odds of dying remain pretty much the same today as yesterday. Death happens, in other words, now as before, with an identical certitude of falling sometime or another on all of us. No one gets out alive. So why this strange persisting silence surrounding the subject? What manner of repression is this, particularly in an age when every other shame barrier has come crashing down? In a Flannery O'Connor story entitled "The Life You Save May Be Your Own",[5] there is this revealing exchange:

> "Why listen, lady," said Mr. Shiftlet with a grin of delight, "the monks of old slept in their coffins."
>
> "They wasn't as advanced as we are," the old woman said.

Some advance. And as for the woman whose sentiment confirms the prejudice of an age, her comeuppance will come soon enough, and in condign fashion, in the form of that same fellow named Mr. Shiftlet, her new son-in-law, whose first conjugal act will be to whisk her retarded daughter off to a distant town and there abandon her to the kindness of strangers. As Eliot observes,

> And the wind shall say: "Here were decent godless people:
> Their only monument the asphalt road
> And a thousand lost golf balls."[6]

Or, again, if we're not careful some of us may come to resemble the character of poor old General Sash, the 104-year-old

---

[5] See her collection of stories *A Good Man Is Hard to Find* — "nine stories about original sin", she called them (New York: Farrar, Straus and Giroux, 1955).

[6] See his "Choruses from 'the Rock'", from *The Complete Poems and Plays: 1909–1950* (New York: Harcourt, Brace and World, 1971), p. 103.

Civil War veteran, whose ironic demise, "in the long line at the Coca-Cola machine", is hilariously told in another O'Connor tale, "A Late Encounter with the Enemy": "Living had got to be such a habit with him that he couldn't conceive of any other condition."[7]

In short, we will have grown so insensibly settled into a mere semblance of life, immured as it were in existence, that we can scarcely conceive of any other state of being. Which may well be why, when Death finally does show up, we're likely to exhibit the look of one "whose sight has suddenly been restored but who finds the light unbearable", to quote yet another O'Connor story, "Greenleaf", which describes an appallingly proud woman, whose fitting fate is to be gored to death by a mad bull. With the bull's head buried deep in the woman's lap — "like a wild tormented lover" — the reader is left with the sense that, in her case at least, nothing less than the most horrific encounter with violent death will serve to awaken

---

7 Also taken from *A Good Man Is Hard to Find.* O'Connor's description is worth reproducing for the light it throws on the condition of one who neither makes things happen nor watches things happen; rather things happen to him. "He had not actually been a general in that war. He had probably been a foot soldier; he didn't remember what he had been; in fact, he didn't remember that war at all. It was like his feet, which hung down now shriveled at the very end of him, without feeling. . . . He didn't remember the Spanish-American War in which he had lost a son; he didn't even remember the son. He didn't have any use for history because he never expected to meet it again" (p. 234). Or this: "He had forgotten history and he didn't intend to remember it again. He had forgotten the name and face of his wife and the names and faces of his children or even if he had a wife and children, and he had forgotten the names of places and the places themselves and what had happened at them" (p. 240). It is instructive to note, apropos of a life so little lived, that, theologically speaking, the condition of so complete a loss of identity, of spiritual amnesia so radical, is Hell.

the woman to the reality of her fallen condition ("a good Christian woman", O'Connor describes her, "with a large respect for religion, though she did not, of course, believe any of it was true"). It is the function of the bull to teach her, and, in fact, by the end of the story the lesson has been learned. The once proud woman, when help finally arrives and the beast whose horns have impaled her is dispatched, "felt the quake in the huge body as it sank, pulling her forward on its head, so that she seemed, when Mr. Greenleaf reached her, to be bent over whispering some last discovery into the animal's ear".[8]

Then there is the poet John Crowe Ransom, who neatly insinuates the same point in his poem "Piazza Piece":

> —I am a gentleman in a dustcoat trying
> To make you hear. Your ears are soft and small
> And listen to an old man not at all,
> They want the young men's whispering and sighing.
> But see the roses on your trellis dying
> And hear the spectral singing of the moon;
> For I must have my lovely lady soon,
> I am gentleman in a dustcoat trying.
>
> —I am a lady young in beauty waiting
> Until my truelove comes, and then we kiss.
> But what grey man among the vines is this
> Whose words are dry and faint as in a dream?
> Back from my trellis, Sir, before I scream!
> I am a lady young in beauty waiting.[9]

---

[8] See her second and final collection of stories, *Everything That Rises Must Converge,* published the year following her death (New York: Farrar, Straus and Giroux, 1965).

[9] See his *Poems and Essays* (New York: Vintage Books, 1955), p. 38.

Yes, she will no doubt scream, for Death, disguised in his grey dustcoat amid the dying roses on her trellis, must surely have his lovely lady. He will not be kept waiting beneath the moon's spectral singing, not even for one who waits on the whispering and sighing of another. "Golden lads and girls all must", Shakespeare says, "As chimney-sweepers, come to dust".[10] There are no exemptions, no loopholes for the lucky few; and so for each of us, "Like as the waves make towards the pebbled shore, / So do our minutes hasten to their end."[11] With each rise and fall of the sea—the dread, implacable sea—we are drawn nearer and nearer to Death. Sooner or later each will utter the same self-styled dirge: "The bright day is done / And we are for the dark."[12]

And when begins the great nightfall? At birth, no less, promised dawn of new life. "We have a winding-sheet in our mother's womb," declares John Donne in a sermon preached before the king, "and we come into the world wound up in that winding-sheet; for we come to seek a grave. . . . We celebrate our funeral with cries, even at our birth."[13]

Man's necessary end is nowhere more terrifyingly told than in the great Tolstoy novella *The Death of Ivan Ilyich,* which has harrowed readers for a hundred years or more with fear and wonder.[14] It is the story of a prosperous and successful man

---

[10] See his *Cymbeline,* act IV, sc. 2. See also Sonnet 35, which strikes the same chord of sad mutability:

> Roses have thorns, and silver fountains mud,
> Clouds and eclipses stain both moon and sun,
> And loathsome canker lives in sweetest bud.

[11] Shakespeare, Sonnet 60.

[12] Shakespeare, *Antony and Cleopatra,* act V, sc. 2.

[13] Cited in C. L. Sulzberger, *Go Gentle into the Night* (in Englewood Cliffs, N.J.: Prentice-Hall, 1976), p. 143.

[14] Leo Tolstoy, *The Death of Ivan Ilyich,* translated by Lynn Solotaroff, with an introduction by Ronald Blythe (New York: Bantam Books, 1981).

of the world who literally cannot confront his own death until the very last, when, beneath the crushing weight of an illness absurdly brought on by a bump sustained while hanging draperies, all pretense and illusion give way. "Can it be true", he asks, "that here, on this drapery, as at the storming of a bastion, I lost my life? How awful and how stupid! It just can't be! It can't be, yet it is."

And for all the suffering he must yet endure, the continual wracking pain of a body in the terminal stages of its own dissolution, the real torment is that no one seems to understand, to admit the stark facts of his approaching annihilation. "Ivan Ilyich suffered most of all from the lie, the lie which, for some reason, everyone accepted: that he was not dying but was simply ill, and that if he stayed calm and underwent treatment he could expect good results. . . . And he was tortured by this lie." Indeed, he longs to lash out at those nearest him, those who, out of some misplaced pity, refuse to acknowledge, to honor, the truth about his own finitude.

> And, oddly enough, many times when they were going through their acts with him he came within a hairbreadth of shouting: "Stop your lying! You and I know that I'm dying, so at least stop lying." But he never had the courage to do it. He saw that the awesome, terrifying act of his dying had been degraded by those about him to the level of a chance unpleasantness, a bit of unseemly behavior (they reacted to him as they would to a man who emitted a foul odor on entering a drawing room); that it had been degraded by that very "propriety" to which he had devoted his entire life.[15]

It is only when propriety itself is stripped away, the careful veneer of an outer wall consisting of appearance and respectability—of a life merely thrown up to keep others and God at

[15] Ibid., p. 103.

bay—that a final honesty may emerge, thus enabling Ivan to face his end with something like dignity and grace. However, it is this self-discovery that occasions the greatest agony of all. "What if my entire life," he asks helplessly near the end, "my entire conscious life, simply was not the real thing?"

> It occurred to him that what had seemed utterly inconceivable before—that he had not lived the kind of life he should have—might in fact be true. . . . His official duties, his manner of life, his family, the values adhered to by people in society and in his profession—all these might not have been the real thing.[16]

This dawning realization of an unreal and unrecollected life, an existence of sheer uninterrupted duplicity, is followed by three days of incessant screaming ("so terrible that even two rooms away one could not hear it without trembling"). Here begins Ivan's final, terrifying descent into the darkness of death, "the black sack into which an unseen, invincible force was thrusting him". And for all his struggling to resist, the instinctive reaction of the condemned prisoner who will not go gently into that good night, Ivan suddenly and ineluctably feels himself drawn to the one thing that he most fears. "He felt he was in agony because he was being shoved into that black hole, but even more because he was unable to get right into it." And of course it is essential to Ivan's peace of soul that he get into that sack.

But what is it that prevents his going forward, the thing such that, until Ivan can bring himself to face it, he cannot embrace his own death? Very simply, it is the illusion that his life has been lived well. The conviction, bred deep in the bone and nourished on countless lies, that his life had been a good one, that all his days had been morally well spent. "This

---

[16] Ibid., pp. 126–27.

justification of his life held him fast, kept him from moving
forward, and caused him more agony than anything else."
Nothing is more necessary in these last hours than that he be
thoroughly disabused of this deceit: " 'Yes, all of it was simply
not the real thing. But no matter. I can still make it the real
thing—I can. But what is the real thing?' Ivan Ilyich asked
himself and suddenly grew quiet."[17]

It is this question that frames the portrait of Ivan's last hours,
the final summation of his life's meaning. It will bring on the
long unlooked-for moment of grace that Ivan, in grasping,
will carry into eternity. Very near the end of an unceasing
ordeal, three days of desperate screaming, Ivan's young son
wanders into the room where the dying man's arms continu-
ally flail about in hapless agony. At once he goes up to his
father and, laying hold of a hand, presses it to his lips and
begins to cry. "At that very moment," says Leo Tolstoy, "Ivan
Ilyich fell through and saw a light, and it was revealed to him
that his life had not been what it should have been but that he
could still rectify the situation."

> "But what is the real thing?" he asked himself and grew quiet,
> listening. Just then he felt someone kissing his hand. He opened
> his eyes and looked at his son. He grieved for him. His wife
> came in and went up to him. He looked at her. She gazed at
> him with an open mouth, with unwiped tears on her nose and
> cheeks, with a look of despair on her face. He grieved for
> her.[18]

It is the realization, made in the presence of death, that in
the end what really matters, what alone matters, is the *quality of
mercy,* the gesture of love, of forgiveness, which we offer to
one another amid the blessed forgetfulness of self. It is Portia's

[17] Ibid., p. 132.
[18] Ibid.

answer to a Shylock madly determined to exact his pound of flesh, the amount that a strict accounting of justice requires. "On what compulsion must I? tell me that", demands old Shylock, who knows the law and his victim's helplessness before its awful logic. Her answer rings out with an eloquence whose seraphic tones reach all the way to Heaven, even if they fail to reach the soul of Shylock, the vindictive moneylender:

> The quality of mercy is not strain'd,
> It droppeth as the gentle rain from heaven
> Upon the place beneath: it is twice blest;
> It blesseth him that gives and him that takes:
> 'Tis mightiest in the mightiest: it becomes
> The throned monarch better than his crown;
> His sceptre shows the force of temporal power,
> The attribute to awe and majesty,
> Wherein doth sit the dread and fear of kings;
> But mercy is above this sceptred sway;
> It is enthroned in the hearts of kings,
> It is an attribute to God himself;
> And earthly power doth then show likest God's
> When mercy seasons justice. Therefore, Jew,
> Though justice be thy plea, consider this,
> That, in the course of justice, none of us
> Should see salvation: we do pray for mercy;
> And that same prayer doth teach us all to render
> The deeds of mercy.[19]

[19] See Shakespeare's *The Merchant of Venice,* act IV, sc. 1. "He shall endure like the sun and the moon from age to age. He shall descend like rain on the meadow, like raindrops on the Earth", to cite Psalm 72, which the Church in her profound wisdom and abysmal need prays during Holy Week to commemorate the events of our Lord's Passion and death, he who is Mercy itself.

"And suddenly it became clear to him that what had been oppressing him and would not leave him suddenly was vanishing all at once—from two sides, ten sides, all sides." And in his solicitude to spare others the suffering that all his life he had thoughtlessly inflicted, Ivan Illych is free to make a good end.

"And death? Where is it?"

He searched for his accustomed fear of death and could not find it. Where was death? What death? There was no fear because there was no death.

Instead of death there was light.

"So that's it!" he exclaimed. "What bliss!"

All this happened in a single moment, but the significance of that moment was lasting. For those present, his agony continued for another two hours. Something rattled in his chest; his emaciated body twitched. Then the rattling and wheezing gradually diminished.

"It is all over," said someone standing beside him.

He heard these words and repeated them in his soul.

"Death is over," he said to himself. "There is no more death."

He drew in a breath, broke off in the middle of it, stretched himself out, and died.[20]

And what is Death? Is it not the distant horn that beckons to us from the dark wood, the wood wherein all fallen pilgrims find themselves lost and alone, where the right road is wholly obscured by sin and error, the road that leads to the longed-for joys of Paradise? Dante, at the beginning of *The Divine Comedy*, awakes in a dark wood, having gone astray from the straight road, and learns to his sorrow that to recover that road will require a steep descent into himself, through hellish awareness of his sins, which, aided by God's grace, will eventually draw him home to Heaven. Only by death to sin and the repentant

[20] Tolstoy, *Death of Ivan Ilyvich*, p. 133–34.

life that follows will he find his way back. Dante, in his drama of the choices men make, the consequences fleshed out for all eternity—whether they be the *cupiditas* of self-love to the exclusion of others or the *caritas* of divine love inclusive of others—has knit together an allegory of sweeping architectural power and brilliance, the sheer grandeur of whose images provides a vast and learned commentary on the Last Things.[21]

And of these the very first ever to be remembered is Death (followed, of course, in the order set down by the old *Penny Catechism,* by Judgment, Hell, and Heaven). "The worst is death, and death will have his day", says Shakespeare in language he ascribes to a despairing king.[22] And the point survives Richard's exaggeration of it: Death as the cessation of that life of which God alone is author is an evil and violent thing. It is the event that takes place the moment the soul, having left the body for

---

[21] See, for example, Dorothy Sayers' incisive analysis of the opening canto from the *Inferno* in which she identifies the chief images and, more to the point, reveals their spiritual and theological significance. "The Dark Wood", she writes, "is the image of Sin and Error—not so much of any specific act of sin or intellectual perversion as of that spiritual condition called 'hardness of heart', in which sinfulness has so taken possession of the soul as to render it incapable of turning to God, or even knowing which way to turn. *The Mountain,* which on the mystical level is the image of the Soul's Ascent to God, is thus on the moral level the image of Repentance, by which the sinner returns to God. It can be ascended directly from "the right road", but not from the Dark Wood, because there the soul's cherished sins have become, as it were, externalized, and appear to it like demons or 'beasts' with a will and power of their own, blocking all progress. Once lost in the Dark Wood, a man can only escape by so descending into himself that he sees his sin, not as an external obstacle, but as the will to chaos and death within him (Hell). Only when he has 'died to sin' can he repent and purge it." The Sayers translation, while less felicitous than others (for instance, John Ciardi or C. H. Sisson), is nevertheless unsurpassed for the quality of its commentary.

[22] *Richard II,* act III, sc. 2.

Judgment, ceases to vivify its functions with the informing, animating principle we call life. The body thus falls away into corruption, leaving the soul to journey across the threshold of eternal life, there to await the moment when God chooses to reconstitute the original body-soul unity for all eternity.

And make no mistake about it: the unity of the two was intended by God from the beginning, man being by definition a psychosomatic unity, a horizon line, as someone once put it, between time and eternity. The promised repatriation of dead body to living soul is what saves us from dualism, that dismal doctrine that splits man in two, thus divesting him of the dignity of his own body, and yields the distinct possibility of personal despair. Who would not court despair knowing half the being he bore was meant for destruction, consigned to some cosmic ash heap? Either body and soul await reunion on the other side or the whole business is a bad joke, man being but animal or angel.

No, death is a historical event each of us lives through right from the beginning. The moment we begin to be we are old enough to die. Death is a constitutive element of our being. Day by day we pass by Death; it is the signpost along the way. We die. That is, in some sense surely, the meaning of life. Of all creatures fashioned by God, man alone carries his Death before him; thus man sees his own Death, the limit of his own finitude, as that final cancelation he must endure, the unraveling of all he might otherwise have done or become. "In death," Hans Urs von Balthasar tells us, "we will forcefully be led from ourselves into total abandonment, because we will be commanded to abandon everything and ourselves."[23]

---

[23] See his *Life out of Death: Meditation on the Easter Mystery* (Philadelphia: Fortress Press, 1985), p. 21. See also Adrienne von Speyr, *The Mystery of Death* (San Francisco: Ignatius Press, 1988), pp. 11–13: "Death

While death is not the last word—and life when framed by the grace of faith needn't be afraid to speak it[24]—there is yet a terrifying finality about man's encounter with death. This is because the moment of death decisively brings to a close the first and most formative phase of human life, indeed, the phase that will prove most determinative of all that will follow. If, as the poet Keats tells us, life is a vale of soul making, that is, a place or setting in which one necessarily gives shape to the soul, that process cannot go on

---

is the end, and as such it is a mystery. It is not the kind of end which is succeeded by a continuation, a reconstruction. It is simply *The End,* complete cessation. God has totally changed man's relation to his life and environment, but he has not told him what he will do with him when life comes to an end. Yet man has some experience of this end: he experiences the death of his fellow men, he sees them being lowered into the earth, he knows that their bodies decompose, that all human contact with them is broken off. No love, no remembrance is able to call them back. Beyond death, coming into view, as it were, in the gap that death leaves, there is only—God. God, who was before this human being existed, who created and accompanied him, who survives his death, just as he will survive my death and the death of every man and of all generations. And what God will do with his deceased creatures is a mystery.... [T]he person who wants to come to God in a relationship of faith does not know what God will do with him. The only certainty he has is that this relationship cannot exempt him from the certainty of death and the uncertainty of the hour. He has no knowledge about possibilities his spirit may have to remain in contact with his flesh; nor does he know whether, when his body disintegrates and returns to its constituent elements, the soul will be able to maintain its relationship with God or be sustained in it by God. Both are equally inconceivable to him."

[24] "Life is eternal", writes Rossiter Worthington Raymond in *A Commendatory Prayer.* "Love is immortal. And death is only a horizon, which is nothing save the limit of our sight" (cited in *Familiar Quotations,* comp. John Bartlett [Boston and Toronto: Little, Brown, 1968], p. 785).

forever. Sooner or later the loom has got to stop and all that we've woven of our lives taken out and shown for what it is. To what does life's attrition point if not a long, drawn-out dying? "For no sooner do we begin to live in this dying body", writes Saint Augustine, "than we begin to move ceaselessly toward death. For in the whole course of this life (if life we must call it) its mutability tends toward death.[25] The place of death, it would thus appear, is imperiously fixed by life itself. The background of a man's life, which is death, gives perspective to all the events of the foreground.

But, again, death is not the end of life. It is, however, the end of the road. At the point of death man has arrived, has reached a certain closure in the journey, and there is nothing more to be done, nowhere else to go. This frail thing, life, which he tenuously holds in his hands ("Between us and Heaven or Hell there is only life half-way," writes Pascal, "the most fragile thing in the world"),[26] this being that God has given man to shepherd, to exercise care and custody of in this body the world, must now give way to something—to Someone—transcendent to himself. From time to eternity: not an easy transaction to make at any time. Yet, if the point of a man's life is finally to get beyond that life, then that pesky stump over there where the road seems to end, to peter out into a kind of blank nothingness ("What did it matter where you lay once you were dead? . . . You slept the big sleep, not caring about the nastiness of

---

[25] Augustine, *The City of God*, bk. XIII, chap. 10.
[26] See his *Pensées*, no. 152.

how you died or where you fell", Raymond Chandler),[27] that stub at the end is no closure at all but rather an opening onto something else, a thing greater and larger than anything we heretofore thought of as life. Death, then, is not a wall against which we fatalistically go smash, falling headlong into a grave others have dug before it; Death is a door through which a man enters upon everlasting life, "a real door leading through a real wall to immortal realities", to recall that enchanting story by H. G. Wells about the man who, haunted all his life by longings no worldly success could assuage, finally appears to walk through that magic opening in the wall.[28] "Old men ought to be explorers", says Eliot.

> Here and there does not matter
> We must be still and still moving
> Into another intensity
> For a further union, a deeper communion
> Through the dark cold and the empty desolation,
> The wave cry, the wind cry, the vast waters
> Of the petrel and the porpoise. In my end is my
> beginning.[29]

And so it is that in life each man will have made something of himself, something to carry across the threshold of death, something he must perforce remain forever after. Of what, after all, does a man's life consist? This strange quintessence of

[27] For readers of genteel literary habit, Raymond Chandler wrote detective fiction of a very high order, of which *The Big Sleep* is among his best. See his *Stories and Early Novels* (New York: Literary Classics of the United States, 1995), pp. 589–764.

[28] See *The Door in the Wall and Other Stories* (Boston: David R. Godine, 1980), pp. 5–24.

[29] From "East Coker", second of Eliot's *Four Quartets*.

dust: What is it for, and whither is it meant to go? Does not the Wisdom literature of the Old Testament, on whose legacy so many dead Masters have drawn for that nourishment of the soul we cannot do without, tell us that life is a thing as vaporous as the dew, which is driven away and disappears with the wind? Or, like the field of grass dried up in the heat of the sun, its relentless withering a datum of our days? "All things have their season," Ecclesiastes tells us, "and in their times all things pass under heaven. A time to be born and a time to die. A time to plant and a time to pluck up that which is planted. A time to kill, and a time to heal . . . to weep . . . to laugh . . . to mourn . . . to dance."[30] So it goes, the endless rhythmic procession of life and death. "Birth, and copulation, and death", writes Eliot in "Sweeny Agonistes", "That's all the facts when you come to brass tacks." And at the end, "you wait for a knock and the turning of a lock for you know the hangman's waiting for you."[31]

And why is that? Because, very simply, man is a being born to die. Or, more to the point, because man alone knows he must die. Animals do not know this; not even in the midst of their dying can they detach themselves sufficiently from the event to meditate on its meaning. It is for man alone to entertain thoughts and fears of impending extinction. Thus death is at once the most commonplace of all happenings; for what could be more banal, more drearily self-evident than the fact of anyone's death? As someone once said, it is only down streets marked by graves that any of us may make our way into the world of the past. But at the same time, is death not also the most painfully incomprehensible, the least tolerable or welcome of all the things that conspire to overtake and destroy

[30] Qo 3:1–6.
[31] See *The Complete Poems and Plays: 1909–1950*, pp. 80–81, 85.

us? "On pain of death, let no man name death to me: It is a word infinitely terrible", to quote the character Braciano, from Webster's *The White Devil,* destined himself for a most horrible end.[32]

In a popular mystery novel by P. D. James, a beautiful stage actress about to be murdered (although she does not know it yet) is asked, "What is it that you're really afraid of?"

"Oh, don't you know ... Death. That's what I'm afraid of. Just death. Stupid, isn't it? I always have been, even when I was a child. I don't remember when it began, but I knew the facts of death before I knew the facts of life. There never was a time when I didn't see the skull beneath the skin. ... It isn't the death of other people. It isn't the fact of death. It's my death I'm afraid of. Not all the time. Not every moment. Sometimes I can go for weeks without thinking about it. And then it comes, usually at night, the dread and the horror and the knowledge that the fear is real. ... It comes in a rhythm, wave after wave of panic sweeping over me, a kind of pain. It must be like giving birth, except that I'm not delivering life. ... Sometimes I hold up my hand, like this, and look at it and think, Here it is, part of me. I can feel it with my other hand, and move it and warm it and smell it and paint its nails. And one day it will hang white and cold and unfeeling and useless, and so shall I be all those things. And then it will rot. And I shall rot. I can't even drink to forget ...

"And it's no good saying that I ought to believe in God. I can't. And even if I could, it wouldn't help."[33]

Can it be any cause for wonder, then, that men flee death, forgetful of the far greater end to which its passing is prelude? For death seemingly "crushes and scatters to the four winds the

[32] From act V, sc. 3.
[33] *The Skull Beneath the Skin* (New York: Charles Scribner, 1982), pp. 109–10.

little bit of meaning that has been laboriously accumulated in a life." Indeed, says Balthasar, death remains the basic "contradiction pervading all existence", a contradiction, he adds, "utterly unresolvable on the purely human level".[34]

Asked once by an interviewer what bothered him most about life, the poet Robert Lowell answered bitterly, "That people die."

"It is the blight man was born for," says the narrator of Gerard Manley Hopkins' haunting poem "Spring and Fall", to the young child who has wandered innocently into the late autumn woods where, weeping but not knowing why, she sadly observes all the fallen leaves die. He asks,

> Margaret, are you grieving
> Over Goldengrove unleaving?
> Leaves, like the things of man, you
> With your fresh thoughts care for. . . .

Alas, he tells her with brutal finality,

> It is Margaret you mourn for.[35]

We must all die, and so, like young Margaret, we are given over to grief at the loss even of the leaves since, in nature's passing, we glimpse the clearest prefiguring of our own. But we are not resigned to die—or to suffer, or to remain always alone—and so we do rage against the dying of the light. Death, solitude, suffering: these things are a problem to us, an outrage even, against the heart of what it means to be human, which is the yearning to live always and in communion with others and without pain. If to be is always to be in relation to others, and to God who is most wholly Other, then Death, to

---

34 Balthasar, *Life out of Death,* pp. 11–12.
35 Hopkins, *Poems,* p. 94.

the extent it severs that web of relationality, can only be an outrage. Death, this thing that rudely intrudes upon and destroys the presence of the other, the beloved other, can only be an unwanted and unlovely thing.

Nevertheless, in a Christian perspective, which is the perspective of grace amid the promised glory to come, death is never simply a phenomenon of nature; it cannot be understood therefore as the mere cessation of bodily being, the clinical collapse and end of *bios* that accompanies life as we know it. For Christianity teaches that in Christ mere *bios* undergoes the unheard-of transforming event of love, thus lifting the life of man, never mind how broken in death, onto the plane of an everlasting life. In short, man's immemorial enemy, which would waylay him to whisk away his life, is outwitted at the very place and pass where one confronts wily death with the force of an unvarying love, thus transmuting the theft and violence sought by death into immeasurable increase of life. The sting of death is at once disarmed by One whose victory is that of an absolute undying love. Thus it is death itself that shall die, to repeat an idea and promise that first found their home in Old Testament hope, where the God of Israel declares to the prophet Hosea, "I will deliver them out of the hand of death. I will redeem them from death: O death, I will be thy death; O Hell, I will be thy bite."[36] It is later given consummate expression in Saint Paul's first Letter to the Corinthians, wherein the majestic chord of Hebrew hope is not just renewed but given lasting guarantee: "For this corruptible must put on incorruption; and this mortal must put on immortality, then shall come to pass the saying that is

---

[36] Hos 13:14.

written: *Death is swallowed up in victory. O death, where is thy sting?*"[37]

Nor may we view the phenomenon of death in accents of chic despair made famous by writers of existentialist *angst.* The late Jean Paul Sartre, for instance, to cite only the most egregious example, once wrote, "It is absurd that we should be born, it is absurd that we shall die." Here is someone for whom death is the terrible annihilating presence awaiting us all, the blank everlasting vacuity we must someday enter. "Nothingness haunts being", he assures us in his principal philosophical work, *Being and Nothingness,* an apt title for the invitation to learned despair it carries. But not to worry: given Monsieur Sartre's mutual absurdity theory, it can scarcely matter either way. "Life," he tells us, "so long as it lasts, is pure and free of any death. For I can conceive of myself only as alive. Man is a being for life, not for death." Here is our old friend Epicurus, the ancient Greek thinker who taught that things are exactly as they appear to the senses. What you see is what you get. Death? What is that to me? he asked scoffingly. "How should I fear death? When I am, death is not; and when death is, I am not." What's the fuss? Why be anxious about that which is not? Well, at least not yet. As Lucretius, Epicurus' brilliant Roman devotee, put it in the century before Christ, and in poetic language so lapidary as to fix the materialist, antimetaphysical canon for all time, "All life is a struggle in the dark." Still, he says, if there be much fear to stalk the human breast, it will all cease upon our death. "If the future holds travail and anguish in store, the self must be in existence, when

---

[37] See his stirring passage in 1 Cor 15:51–58. Donne, in Sonnet X, admirably renders the original in his own inimitable way:

> One short sleep past, we wake eternally;
> And death shall be no more; death thou shalt die.

that time comes, in order to experience it. But from this fate we are redeemed by death, which denies existence to the self that might have suffered these tribulations. Rest assured, therefore, that we have nothing to fear in death. One who no longer is cannot suffer."[38]

No, the Christian view of death is that it can only finally be understood in theological terms, as an event intelligible only in the light of faith trained on the deposit of God's Revelation, the saving Word that is Jesus Christ. Saint Paul, as always, has the sense of it. "Therefore," he writes, "as sin came into the world through one man and death through sin, and so death spread to all men because all men sinned."[39] The source of death is not any sort of inner necessity of human nature; rather, it is the result of sin, the sin of Adam and Eve, the original sin, which Newman has called "the aboriginal calamity".

Death is found in the opening pages of the book of Genesis, the formative text that will in turn launch the whole Hebrew and Christian understanding of God and man. And the narrative of what went wrong in the Garden is perhaps worth reproducing, for it is here that death, the smirking skull beneath the skin, makes his first formal appearance.

> And the Lord God planted a garden in Eden, in the east; and He placed there the man whom He had formed. Out of the ground the Lord God made various trees grow that were delightful to look at and good for food, with the tree of life in the middle of the garden and the tree of the knowledge of good and evil. . . . The Lord God took the man and put him in the garden of Eden to till it and keep it. And the Lord God

[38] See his *On the Nature of the Universe* (London: Penguin, 1951), p. 122. Lucretius of course is the great and poetic exegete of Epicurus, who preached only the evidence of the senses, behind which even the smirking skull of Death could not dismay.

[39] Rom 5:12.

commanded the man, saying, "You may freely eat of every tree of the garden; but of the tree of the knowledge of good and evil you shall not eat, for in that day that you eat of it you shall die."[40]

Thereupon the serpent, we are told, with that devilish cunning of which fallen man is now only too sadly aware, tells the woman whom he has sought out in order to deceive that, no, she will most definitely not die. "For God knows that when you eat of it your eyes will be opened, and you will be like God, knowing good and evil."[41] So begins the long saga of sin and suffering, man's fall and dishonor founded upon a lie.

If death, then, is not constitutive of man's essential being, does not belong to the order of nature at all but rather of history, it follows that God, from the beginning, never intended that man should die. "For God created man for incorruption", the book of Wisdom tells us, "and made him in the image of His own eternity, but through the devil's envy death entered the world, and those who belong to his party experience it."[42]

Death, for all the harrowing finality of its fall into the weakness and futility of being human, for all that it shatters of the original body-soul unity, death nevertheless belongs to the order of that history bloodied by sin that God himself suffered to enter and redeem. For the gift of grace, as the whole Pauline corpus reminds us, is not at all like the sin of the law. "For if by the offense of one man all died," he writes in Romans, "much more did the grace of God and the gracious gift of the one man, Jesus Christ, abound for all."[43]

[40] Gen 2:8–9, 15–17.
[41] Gen 3:4–5.
[42] Wis 2:23–24.
[43] Rom 5:15.

Thus Christ undertook to assume our death in order precisely to deliver us from the absurdity of it. "The Christian who unites his own death to that of Jesus views it as a step towards him and an entrance into everlasting life", says the *Catechism of the Catholic Church.*[44] And why is this? Because when Christ died, something extraordinary happened to death that fundamentally changes the whole dismal equation of sin and Death. In death, God calls man to himself. Therefore the Christian can experience a desire for Death like the one Saint Paul records in his letter to the Philippians: "My desire is to depart and be with Christ."[45] Thus for the Christian whose life is an effort to cleave to Christ, to anchor all hope in him who came to conquer sin and death, the "victory" of Death is only apparent. "So death will come to fetch you?" asks Saint Thérèse of Lisieux. "No, not death, but God Himself. Death is not the horrible spectre we see represented in pictures. The catechism teaches that death is the separation of the soul from the body; that is all. I am not afraid of a separation which will unite me forever with God."[46]

44 CCC, 1020.

45 Phil 1:21.

46 See her "Counsels and Memories", cited in *Death: A Book of Preparation and Consolation,* edited and compiled by Barry Ulanov (New York: Sheed and Ward, 1959), p. 22.

Judgment

At the moment of any man's death—that is, at his passing out of this world, and never mind for now the medical perplexities of trying to determine the exact moment when it happens— the ambit of human activity, human liberty, is ended. There is nothing more to be done. The play is over, time's theater closed. Devouring time, that "bloody tyrant" Shakespeare calls it, has done his worst, and man lies prostrate before his feet. The life that each man has lived, the life that even now has ended and is no more, that life is replete with all the meaning it will ever have. In the event of each man's death, there will crystallize the full measure of life's significance, the distilled weight and value of its eternal worth.

Then, at the appointed close of that period allotted to each of us by God, a period in which an all-wise and merciful Providence allows us time for the free exercise of the will (whether for good or ill is not yet in question), each of us will step out from behind the wings of this world, and there, on the other side, across the threshold of death, be ushered into fiery collision with Ultimate Reality itself, the very *Pantokrator* in whose blazing presence everlasting Judgment falls on every man who has ever lived. An eternity of loss or gain, no less, awaiting the entire human race. "The boast of heraldry," writes Thomas Gray, "the pomp of power, / And all that beauty, all that wealth e'er gave / Awaits alike the inevitable hour: / The paths of glory lead but to the grave."[1] Thus do we all go to that hour of Judgment that none can gainsay.

Now it is a datum of Christian faith, the maintenance of which is central to the truth Christ came into the world to preach and defend, that despite the fact of Death, our Death, God is nevertheless good. He is not the author of Death, the wicked Demiurge of man's undoing. Moreover, we Christians believe that he alone is good; there is none whose goodness does not derive from his own inexhaustible supply. We are not Manicheans, who must boringly divide up our divinities according to whether or not they emit light or dark, good or evil. The Christian God is entirely devoid of darkness, unless it be that "dazzling darkness" of which the mystics speak; and, as for goodness, he is the fullness thereof. When the rich young man accosted Christ to ask what must he do to inherit eternal life, he correctly addressed Christ as "good Master". Jesus does not contradict him. "Why do you call me good? No one is good

---

[1] These are lines taken from that famous late eighteenth-century masterpiece "Elegy Written in a Country Churchyard", whose mournful tones reverberate throughout so much of nineteenth-century lyric reflection on Death. It is a poem of exquisite melancholy on the subject, specifically the passing of so many quiet, unassuming country folk, their simple lives lived "far from the madding crowd's ignoble strife".

> Can storied urn or animated bust
>   Back to its mansion call the fleeting breath?
> Can Honor's voice provoke the silent dust,
>   Or flattery soothe the dull cold ear of Death?
>
> Full many a gem of purest ray serene
>   The dark unfathomed caves of ocean bear;
> Full many a flower is born to blush unseen,
>   And waste its sweetness on the desert air.

but God alone."[2] Christ, who is God, is surely entitled to wear the crown of goodness.

The good, then, is not a standard by which we set about assessing God, a banner held aloft the Supreme Being, a placard flapping in the face of Alpha and Omega. To think so is to fall into Platonism, a species of dreary essentialism in which the Forms or Ideas themselves transcend God, standing in timeless judgment upon the Creator and Redeemer of the world. No, goodness is not some absolute measure waiting to be applied to anything in, or even above, the cosmos. It is certainly not any sort of Procrustean bed on which God himself must be made to fit. When Jesus admonishes his followers not to judge lest they be judged, "For the measure you give will be the measure you get back",[3] what can it mean for him? Is he not the measure itself, whose giving out and getting back are entirely of a piece with his own eternal and absolute being? Goodness is simply another name we apply to God; it is one of countless predications of his nature, like truth or holiness or mercy. God cannot, as it were, help himself from either being good or doing good. Goodness is thus God himself, both in being and doing.

And if God alone is good, if his nature and dealings with men are characterized that way, then it becomes a necessary exercise of his will that we too do good in order that, like him, we might also become good. More to the point, that we become perfect, even as our Father in Heaven is perfect. Thus we may say, in the language of the Psalmist, "The Lord is my inheritance and my cup; He alone will give me my reward. The measuring line has marked a lovely place for me; my

2 Mk 10:18.
3 Mt 7:2.

inheritance is my great delight."[4] How could God mark out such a place if he were not himself the measure?

Still, God is scarcely in a position to enforce the goodness he enjoins. Not in this world he isn't. His unspeakably pure, transcendently holy will may be the highest law in the world, conformity to which will infallibly bring happiness and peace in this world and the next. "In His will is our peace", says Dante in the *Commedia*.[5] But provision having been made for human choice, for that liberty befitting men made in his image, we are likewise free to despise and reject his holy will, to disdain the good God himself. In other words, man is subject to Judgment.

"The Law is given that grace may be sought", Augustine tells us. "And grace is given that the Law may be fulfilled." Suppose man chooses neither to seek nor to find. Suppose he chooses to stand athwart both grace and the Law. Will God strike him dead? Will the earth, repelled by his wickedness, swallow him whole? Of course not. God having literally set men free to spit in his face — "the intolerable compliment", C. S. Lewis calls it, whereby Divine Omnipotence pays mankind the highest possible compliment of taking its liberty seriously — he will not revoke the gift, will not even regret having given it.[6] "God put His hope in us", writes Charles Péguy in a

---

4 Ps 16.

5 From the *Paradiso,* canto III, l. 85.

6 "I might, indeed, have learned, even from the poets," he writes in *The Problem of Pain,* "that Love is something more stern and splendid than mere kindness: that even the love between the sexes is, as in Dante, 'a lord of terrible aspect.' There is kindness in Love: but Love and kindness are not coterminous, and when kindness . . . is separated from the other elements of Love, it involves a certain fundamental indifference to its object. . . . [W]e have all met people whose kindness to animals is constantly leading them to kill animals lest they should suffer. Kindness, merely as

daring series of verses on the virtue and mystery of hope. "He took the initiative. He hoped that the least / of the sinners, / That the tiniest of the sinners would at least work a little for his salvation."

God is the *hoper* who comes in hope for us men, hoping we might bestir ourselves a wee bit on behalf of our own salvation. What an astonishing idea! "You must have confidence in God", says Péguy, "He certainly has had / confidence in us. / He had enough confidence in us to give us, to entrust us with his only / Son. / (Alas alas what we did with Him.)"[7]

We have certainly returned the favor. "If a game is played," Lewis reminds us, "it must be possible to lose it. If the happiness of a creature lies in self-surrender, no one can make that surrender but himself (though many can help him to make it) and he may refuse."[8] It is the whole screaming paradox of salvation: freely offered by One who despite being infinitely fetching, infinitely irresistible, will yet not overcome man's

---

such, cares not whether its object becomes good or bad, provided only that it escapes suffering. As Scripture points out, it is bastards who are spoiled: the legitimate sons, who are to carry on the family tradition, are punished. It is for people whom we care nothing about that we demand happiness on any terms: with our friends, our lovers, our children, we are exacting and would rather see them suffer much than be happy in contemptible and estranging modes. If God is Love, He is, by definition, something more than mere kindness. And it appears, from all the records, that though He has often rebuked us and condemned us, He has never regarded us with contempt. He has paid us the intolerable compliment of loving us, in the deepest, most tragic, most inexorable sense." (New York: Macmillan, 1972), pp. 40–41.

7 From *The Portal of the Mystery of the Second Virtue,* written shortly after Péguy's return to the Church in 1907. See *Communio* 21 (Fall 1994): 504–25.

8 Lewis, *Problem of Pain,* p. 118.

freedom to resist, his right not to be fetched. Lewis, while
making the point that each of us is a Divine work of art—
"something that God is making, and therefore something with
which He will not be satisfied until it has a certain character"[9]
—must nevertheless concede that in the case of this work
of art, the soul of man wrought by God, the canvas be
left free to resist the brush strokes of its Artist. What could
be more extraordinary? God, whom we are told is easily
pleased, albeit seldom satisfied, must thus suffer the perversity, in this life anyhow, of an upstart creature refusing even
that adornment that will perfect its being for all eternity.
Such is the nature and scope of an unbridled liberty, the
power to choose its own destruction, to carry itself straight
into Hell.

And no doubt, says Lewis, the objection can be made that
given the loss of even one soul, its trajectory propelling it
inexorably into hellish darkness and doom, Divine Omnipotence has lost, is defeated. And the objection carries.

> In creating beings with free will, omnipotence from the outset
> submits to the possibility of such defeat . . . to make things
> which are not Itself, and thus to become, in a sense, capable of
> being resisted by its own handiwork, is the most astonishing
> and unimaginable of all the feats we attribute to the Deity. I
> willingly believe that the damned are, in one sense, successful,
> rebels to the end; that the doors of Hell are locked on the
> *inside.*"[10]

9 "We are, not metaphorically but in very truth, a Divine work
of art, something that God is making, and therefore something with
which He will not be satisfied until it has a certain character. Here
again we come up against what I have called the 'intolerable compliment' " (ibid., p. 42).

10 Ibid., p. 127.

Whether in fact any of us will actually go there, slamming his door of Hell in God's face, is of course the whole point that the second of the Four Last Things is meant to determine. The Judgment put off due to this strange powerlessness of the Judge, who intensely wills the good in this life but does not compel any of us to do it, all that will be different following the hour of our death. The Lord of life and history, the mystery of whose willed impotence is such that he may only urge and entreat us to accept the truth, never force it upon us, that state of affairs will not persist into eternity. Then the window of earthly opportunity will have shut forever. "Now God", as Romano Guardini puts it, "confronts man in His Holy Essence. Sovereign Goodness is one with irresistible power. God wills with divine intensity that good be realized. The look He casts on man becomes the Judgment, a Judgment that determines man's true being and the shape of his eternal destiny. All this is meant by the words 'God judges'."[11]

And, of course, as all Scripture and Tradition tell us, and the testimony of the dead can verify ("And what the dead had no speech for, when living, / They can tell you, being dead: the communication / Of the dead is tongued with fire beyond the language of the / living," writes Eliot),[12] the Judgment spoken by God is final, a sentence from which there can be no appeal. To whom, indeed, could any further appeal be made? What higher agency is there besides God to which the soul can turn? There is no Other, and none greater, than he who is Lord of All. He who first drew the universe out of nothingness, then slew the powers of darkness and death that sought to unravel

[11] *The Last Things* (New York: Pantheon Books, 1954), p. 34.
[12] See Eliot's first movement of "Little Gidding", the last of his *Four Quartets*.

the work of his hand—the dual handiwork of creation and covenant, by which we men are both given and forgiven—he alone exists to whom a redress of sentence might be made. And his Judgment is final, unalterable. As the Fourth Lateran Council put it in 1215, pursuant to setting the record straight on what Christianity actually believes about the resurrection of the body and life after death, robustly asserting in the teeth of the errors of Albigensianism then threatening to undermine the faith, "He [Christ] will come at the end of the world; he will judge the living and the dead; and he will reward all, both the lost and the elect, according to their works. And all these will rise with their own bodies which they now have so that they may receive according to their works, whether good or bad; the wicked, a perpetual punishment with the devil; the good, eternal glory with Christ."[13]

Thus Judgment at the last will take but one of two unending forms: Salvation or Damnation. Perdition or Paradise. One or the other awaits all men at the Final Trumps. There can be no Third Way for those equally averse to going to either place, that is, disdaining both Heaven *and* Hell, a scenario that Dante apparently spins out in the early cantos of his *Inferno,* where in the Vestibule of Hell one encounters the Futile, their fate to race forever after a whirling standard symbolizing the choices they never made. "Who against God rebelled not, nor to Him / Were faithful, but to self alone were true".[14] Dante is pitiless in assessing their predicament, the wretched souls of men whose weather-cock minds shrink from making one decision lest it preclude another. "Heaven cast them forth", he

---

[13] See *The Church Teaches: Documents of the Church in English Translation* (Rockford, IL: Tan Books, 1973), p. 347.

[14] See canto III, the *Inferno,* ll. 38–39, translated by Dorothy Sayers (Baltimore, Md.: Penguin Classics, 1976), p. 86.

writes, "their presence there would dim the light; / deep Hell rejects so base a herd, / Lest sin should boast itself because of them."[15]

Leaving aside a certain poetic license in Dante's imaginative reconstruction of the Underworld, which enables him to consign numberless souls to the City of Desolation ("I had not thought death had undone so many"),[16] souls whose only sin appears to be their refusal to commit any, Dante's point is surely the orthodox one that in the end not to choose is really a form of choice. As Dorothy Sayers puts it in her learned and delightful commentary, "Heaven and Hell being states in which choice is permanently fixed, there must also be a state in which the refusal of choice is itself fixed, since to refuse choice is in fact to choose indecision."[17]

And so the only finally available choices reduce to two, toward which even now each member of the human race is moving, some perhaps more quickly than others. The first is prefaced by those words no more terrifying than which can be imagined: "Depart from Me, ye cursed, into everlasting

[15] Ibid., ll 40–42.

[16] See Eliot's variation on the theme in *The Wasteland,* perhaps *the* poetic keystone to an understanding of twentieth-century ennui, where, at the close of the first movement, "The Burial of the Dead", he writes:

> Unreal City,
> Under the brown fog of a winter dawn,
> A crowd flowed over London Bridge, so many,
> I had not thought death had undone so many.

[17] "The Vestibule (which is where Dante contemptuously tosses the Trimmers) is the abode of the weather-cock mind, the vague tolerance which will neither approve nor condemn, the cautious cowardice for which no decision is ever final. The spirits rush aimlessly after the aimlessly whirling banner, stung and goaded, as of old, by the thought that, in doing anything definite whatsoever, they are missing doing something else" (p. 89).

fire which was prepared for the devil and his angels."[18] The second is that promised deliverance, however long delayed by refining purgatorial fire, into the arms and heart of God. "In the end," as C. S. Lewis reminds us in that magnificent sermon "The Weight of Glory", which he preached at Oxford in 1941, "that Face which is the delight or the terror of the universe must be turned upon each of us either with one expression or with the other, either conferring glory inexpressible or inflicting shame that can never be cured or disguised."[19]

Indeed, as Lewis elsewhere tries to imagine the scene as it might well transpire before the tribunal of Almighty God, in which (again) there can be only two kinds of people, he suggests that either the creature will say to God, "Thy will be done", or God will say to the creature, "*Thy* will be done."[20] Whoever goes to Hell takes himself there, including even those whom Dante has contemptuously called the "trimmers", who set their miserable sails to the prevailing wind because in the end they seem not to want to go anywhere. One is either prepared to accept God and the rules of the game he wrote ("The moral is, it is indeed," says Hillaire Belloc, "thou shalt not monkey with the Creed") or set about living the lie of writing one's own rules (the loss of "the good of intellect", Aristotle calls it, which is truth, that is, God, which loss Dante ascribes to all the lost souls) and so face rejection by God. "All that are in Hell choose it. Without that self-choice," says Lewis, "there could be no Hell. No soul that seriously and constantly desires joy will ever miss it. Those who seek find. To those who knock it is opened."[21] In other words, there is no Third Way.

[18] Mt 25:41.

[19] See his *Weight of Glory,* p. 10.

[20] See his superb allegory, *The Great Divorce* (New York: Macmillan, 1946), p. 72.

[21] Ibid., pp. 72–73.

And so final sentence is imposed, to which no appeal can be made to overturn. Because the verdict given is the truth, and truth alone is triumphant, there can be no possible vanquishing of its force or clarity, no mistaking of what it all finally means. "In death," writes Joseph Ratzinger, "a human being emerges into the light of full reality and truth. He takes up that place which is truly his by right. The masquerade of living with its constant retreat behind posturings and fictions, is now over. Man is what he is in truth. Judgment consists in this removal of the mask in death. The judgment is simply the manifestation of the truth."[22] When a man leaves behind the company of other men, the society and life he knew and loved in this world, and walks toward the seat of divine Judgment, there to gaze upon the Face of the living God, all pretense and falsehood are stripped away. In answering to God alone, which is what Judgment means (one cannot dispatch an attorney into that courtroom: "Here, you take the case!"), there is no room for maneuver, no way to disguise the weight of what one has done or become in the world. Then the true worth of a man's deeds, whether empty straw or solid metal, will be shown in an absolutely piercing light, which is God himself.

Who else, then, but the Son, the Second Person of the Blessed Trinity—Word, Logos himself—is fit to speak this truth? Only Christ is endowed with a sufficiency of truth (he who is truth) to deliver that final and irrevocable sentence. "The heart is deceitful above all things", declares the prophet Jeremiah, "and desperately corrupt. Who can understand it?"[23] There is only One who can give answer to that question, the

---

[22] See Joseph Ratzinger, *Eschatology—Death and Eternal Life,* trans. Michael Waldstein (Washington, D.C.: Catholic University of America Press, 1988), p. 206.

[23] Jer 17:9.

question that haunts Old and New Testaments alike. "I the
Lord search the mind and try the heart, to give to every man
according to his ways, according to the fruit of his doings."[24]
Thus it is that God's Judgment, his Word, bears an ultimacy
that nothing in this world can outweigh. Indeed, Jesus himself
tells us, "For judgment I came into this world."[25] Does it not
follow that only the One who is at the heart of the world can
know and judge the heart of man? The Father disclaims all
Judgment, we are told, but only because he has given it all over
to the Son, "that all may honor the Son, even as they honor
the Father".

> He who does not honor the Son does not honor the Father
> who sent Him. Verily, verily, I say to you, he who hears My
> word and believes Him who sent Me has eternal life; he does
> not come into judgment, but has passed from death to life.
> Verily, verily, I say to you, the hour is coming, and now is,
> when the dead will hear the voice of the Son of God, and those
> who hear will live. For as the Father has life in Himself, so He
> has granted the Son also to have life in Himself, and has given
> Him authority to execute judgment, because He is the Son of
> man. Do not marvel at this; for the hour is coming when all
> who are in the tombs will hear His voice and come forth, those
> who have done good, to the resurrection of life, and those who
> have done evil, to the resurrection of judgment.[26]

Surely the Scriptures provide ample warning of the Judgment to come? In the book of Sirach we are succinctly told,
"In all you do, remember the end of your life, and then you
will never sin."[27] But, alas, how few of us there are who do

[24] Jer 17:10.
[25] Jn 9:39.
[26] Jn 5:22–29.
[27] Sir 7:36.

remember; and, again, we are all free to forget. What else is human history but an endless and culpable number of acts of human forgetfulness, of men and women who, having forgotten the lessons of one generation, are thus condemned to repeat them in the next? How high that great dust heap we call history is piled with the sins of dead men. Gibbon was right that history is "little more than the register of the crimes, follies, and misfortunes of mankind".[28] So what is God to do with those of us who make history? (And we all make it, however circumscribed the arenas of our mischief.) Will he not make the wicked and the perverse pay for their crimes and follies? "Christ warns us that we must answer for what we have received", François Mauriac writes. "When it is Himself we have received, what shall we not have to answer for?"[29] (Again, that "intolerable compliment" God pays to the race of men, the race into whose midst God's Son appears, breaking himself to become our Bread.)

This much, then, should be clear: that God's will to redeem an entire world steeped in sin, reprobate right down to the bottom of its being, cannot be certain of success in every case. Remember, it is in hope that we are saved, not certainty. So what is God to do with those who appear obdurate to the end? Hardened sinners who, by the twisted turn of their lives—their souls pretzel shaped from years of perversity—refuse even their own salvation? He cannot very well grab them by the seat of their pants and pull them kicking and screaming into the Precincts of Joy and Felicity, can he? Not without their consent he can't. And if they choose not to consent? "I will not

---

[28] See chapter II of his monumental *Decline and Fall of the Roman Empire*.

[29] See his *The Eucharist: The Mystery of Holy Thursday* (New York and Toronto: Longham, Green, 1945), pp. 56–57. See also Lk 12:48: "Every one to whom much is given, of him will much be required."

serve" is not only the motto of demonic disobedience, it is every sinner's signature. And God will not force the letters to go another way; his writing straight with crooked lines presupposes our willingness to submit to revision.

The conclusion is inescapable: where a man's life remains seriously at variance to God's, to that vision of happiness that from all eternity God has scripted for man—a life, indeed, that stands in continual and even monstrous contradiction to God's Law, the structures of which he wisely inscribes in man's nature in order that he might freely conform to his Law—what recourse does that exactly leave God save Judgment upon the sins of man? "I have not come to judge the world but to save it", declares Jesus. "He who rejects me and does not receive my sayings has a judge; the word that I have spoken will be his judge on the last day."[30] In short, to quote the passage from Traherne, whom Lewis cites in his *Problem of Pain,* "Love can forbear, and Love can forgive . . . but Love can never be reconciled to an unlovely object. . . . He can never therefore be reconciled to your sin, because sin itself is incapable of being altered; but He may be reconciled to your person, because that may be restored."[31]

However, it is not only God who will judge the sinner, confronting him with the record of his life in order to determine the place where he will spend all eternity—the Judge musing aloud, as it were, on the iniquities of his creatures, wondering which if any will escape the net of retribution: "Hmm, let me see now . . . is it to be a final, infernal fall into the torments of Hell, the condemned soul before my Face, whose countenance so often in this life he'd disfigured by sin, hearing those horrific and appalling words I've so often rehearsed with other sinners: 'I never knew you. Depart from me forever'?

[30] Jn 12:47–48.
[31] Lewis, *Problem of Pain,* p. 37.

Or will perhaps there be a bit of Mercy instead? 'Come, O fortunate soul whom I now honor and invite into my House, there to shine like the sun for all ages, basking in the glory of an Eternal Son.' What shall it be today?" Yes, and every day since, as Lewis warns, "we walk on the razor edge between these two incredible possibilities.... All day long we are, in some degree, helping each other to one or other of these destinations."[32]

No, it is not simply God fixing a man's destiny for forever. Man too longs for that rendering of his true worth. Even the greatest of sinners will call out at the last for justice, albeit at his own expense and athwart his own perverse will. "In the final analysis," writes Ratzinger, "man becomes his own judgment."[33] It is not Christ, he reminds us, who dispenses damnation; hurling people into Hell is not his business at all. Rather, we take ourselves there by setting limits on his offer of salvation.

> Christ inflicts pure perdition on no one. In Himself He is sheer salvation. Anyone who is with Him has entered the space of deliverance and salvation. Perdition is not imposed by Him, but comes to be wherever a person distances himself from Christ. It comes about whenever someone remains enclosed within himself. Christ's word, the bearer of the offer of salvation, then lays bare the fact that the person who is lost has himself drawn the dividing line and separated himself from salvation.[34]

Alas, it is a line many of us have drawn often enough already. Faith tells us, and repeated experience easily confirms the telling, that we are free to persist in the drawing of that line; indeed, we may extend it all the way to Hell. And what is

---

[32] Lewis, *Weight of Glory and Other Addresses* (Grand Rapids, Mich.: Eerdmans, 1977), pp. 12 and 15.

[33] Ratzinger, *Eschatology*, p. 207.

[34] Ibid., pp. 205–6.

Hell? It is not other people, as Sartre spuriously supposed in
No Exit. It is being alone, absolutely and forever. Hell is the
condition of a man who, having habituated himself to a life
of complete self-enclosure, announces forever before God, "I
don't want to love. I don't want to be loved. Just leave me to
myself."[35] It is a Judgment that the unrepentant sinner will
himself have made; God is there merely to ratify the truth of
what it really means.

It all begins here and now, in this time and place. "Even
now," says Ratzinger, "in our decision as between faith and
nonfaith, judgment falls."[36] Chesterton provides a wonderful
example of this in his own life when, in response to a newspaper survey asking its readers to answer the question "What's
wrong with the world?", he replied at once, "I am." Whatever
else men have believed—and such a bewildering array it has
been! —they have all believed there is something the matter
with men. Indeed, there is a worm in the human heart whose
poison, when left to seep into the life of man, will eventually
lay waste the world. All life is allegory, a story emblematic of
good and evil, and every age is understood best by parable.
Ours is singularly lacking in a sense of judgment, despite the
great weight of his own, which hovers about our pretensions
like a terrible cloud of storm threatening at any moment to
burst.

The philosopher Maritain observed once that the artist and
God have at least this much in common, that while they love
their creations they will nevertheless judge them without

[35] A very wise Jesuit priest, Fr. Herbert Alphonso, director of the
Ignatian Spirituality Center in Rome, described Hell in just those terms,
while conducting "an intensive initiation into the study of the text of the
Spiritual Exercises" some years ago.
[36] See his *Eschatology,* p. 205.

sentimentality. The modern tendency is to exude the sentiment but withhold the judgment. Yet the artist or writer who refuses to begin with the reality of the mystery of original sin, what Pascal called the one mystery in the absence of which all else is mystery (the one doctrine, Chesterton tells us, the Church never needed to defend, evidence for which having been strewn about everywhere—"as practical as potatoes", he said), cannot be trusted. Because to circumvent the drama of sin in a story that aims to tell the truth about men, an imaginative rendering of real human experience, is in effect to detach art from life, which is of course full of sin. And suffering and Death and, yes, Judgment.

"Fiction is the most impure and the most modest and the most human of the arts", writes Flannery O'Connor, who practiced the art with an almost lapidary perfection. "It is closest to man in his sin and his suffering and his hope."[37] When her friend Walker Percy won the National Book Award in 1962, reporters wanted to know why so many fine Southern writers dominated the field (Percy himself being from Louisiana). Percy's answer was, "Because we lost the war". What Percy meant is something more profound than that a defeated people are more likely to tell better stories. What he meant was that losing the war implied that the South had had its Fall; it had suffered a terrible loss of innocence, of imagined self-sufficiency. Here was a whole people suddenly uprooted from its illusions; thrust by violence into that peculiar drama of salvation history in which the Children of Pride suffer chastisement from their God, whose awful wrath is poured out upon the land. In the midst of an emergent and triumphant modern world where Yankee and secularist values were in the saddle, the South

[37] See her astonishing collection of essays entitled *Mystery and Manners* (New York: Farrar, Straus and Giroux, 1962), p. 192.

found itself suddenly seared with the knowledge of good and evil, of human folly and sin; "with an inborn knowledge of human limitations and with a sense of mystery which could not have developed in our first state of innocence" is how O'Connor would put it. In short, the South and its people stood in Judgment before the Lord.[38]

It is a knowledge singularly religious and salutary, concerning which the rest of the country seems largely to have been spared. The results have proven to be impoverishing in the extreme; those who miss the experience are blighted in some real if undefined way. In an interview some years later Percy predicted, somewhat ruefully one suspects, that in the future it would be the writers of fiction, and not the new theologians, who would remain the only surviving witness to the doctrine of original sin. Certainly in his own stories sin is never far removed from the action of his characters, all of whom live and move in a world, as Saint Paul assures us, groaning under the weight of the "mystery of iniquity".[39] In fact, he would insist, the wages of sin, the wounded human condition, is where every honest writer must begin; and all that he does in the way of development—of character, plot, theme—should leave the reader with the sense of what he calls "the imminence of catastrophe in paradise". It is a word whose use here is obviously ironic, intended to describe the modern world, that lotus land of desperately shallow suburban good cheer. It is also where O'Connor begins, however rural and poor the outward setting of her stories. And why they seem so fantastically filled with freaks, with the poor and the crippled and the unlovely, all the afflicted of mind and soul, who dwell amid

[38] Ibid., p. 59.
[39] 2 Thes 2:7, KJV.

"the dark city where the children of God lay sleeping". When asked why so many Southern writers, herself especially, were always putting freaks in their fiction, she answered, "Because we're still able to recognize one."

> To be able to recognize a freak, you have to have some conception of the whole man, and in the South the general conception of man is still, in the main, theological ... while the South is hardly Christ-centered, it is most certainly Christ-haunted. The Southerner, who isn't convinced of it, is very much afraid that he may have been formed in the image and likeness of God ... it is when the freak can be sensed as a figure for our essential displacement that he attains some depth in literature.[40]

With much of America positively awash in ersatz innocence, abundance, and success, it is good to see a token or two of regional resistance. "Because we lost the war."

But for that war, the chosen instrument of a catastrophic civil war, God might never have succeeded in penetrating the hard shell of a people's complacency and conceit, qualities so characteristic of a society steeped in righteous unrepentance before the terrible injustice of slavery. Of course, not every lost war will have this effect, but in the South, where the levels of literary achievement have been astonishingly and disproportionately high, the best writers were always possessed of a kind of double blessing (the phrase is Flannery O'Connor's), to wit, a lost war, a shattered innocence, and a deep theological sensitivity to the meaning of it all. "Behind our own history," she writes, "deepening it at every point, has been another history. . . . In the South we have, in however attenuated a

[40] See her essay "The Grotesque in Southern Fiction", included in *Mystery and Manners*, pp. 44–45.

form, a vision of the face of Moses as he pulverized our idols."[41]

What a splendid image that is! So wonderfully evocative of O'Connor's work, her stories, which evince this marvelous gift she had for seeing in a regional history, a rural setting, the light of a universal truth. Let belief, she said, be the light by which the artist sees, but do not presume to allow it to replace the act of seeing itself. "For the writer of fiction, everything has its testing point in the eye, and the eye is the organ that eventually involves the whole personality, and as much of the world as can be got into it. It involves judgment. Judgment is something that begins in the act of vision, and when it does not, or when it becomes separated from vision, then a confusion exists in the mind which transfers itself to the story."[42] There was no such confusion in O'Connor's mind, whose eye was limpid and bright, full of prophetic judgment that enabled her to penetrate the concrete world in order, as she put it, "to find at its depths the image of its source, the image of ultimate reality". Prophecy, she insisted, "is a matter of seeing near things with their extensions of meaning and thus of seeing far things close up. The prophet is a realist of distances."[43] Like the blind man in the Gospel, he sees other men as though they were trees, but walking. Where, then, is the writer of stories meant to locate his craft? Let him operate, she said, "at that

[41] "This knowledge is what makes the Georgia writer different from the writer from Hollywood or New York. It is the knowledge that the novelist finds in his community. When he ceases to find it there, he will cease to write, or at least he will cease to write anything enduring. The writer operates at a peculiar crossroads where time and place and eternity somehow meet. His problem is to find that location." From her essay "The Regional Writer", p. 59.

[42] O'Connor, *Mystery and Manners*, p. 91.

[43] Ibid., p. 44.

peculiar crossroads where time and eternity somehow meet". It is the point of intersection, of which the poet Eliot speaks, the Christic point, where all polarities—time/eternity, nature/grace, God/man—converge.

Seeing everything in relation to that Christic point, making the action of character reveal as much of the mystery of Christ as vision and craft permit, that is what finally accounts for so many luminous epiphanies of grace and meaning—and Judgment!—arising out of the concrete particulars confronting the characters in O'Connor's stories. For instance, Mrs. Shortley, a woman of blind bigotry and overweening pride, whom we meet right at the beginning of one such story. It is called "The Displaced Person", the impacted ironies of which will not be lost on the attentive reader. "She stood on two tremendous legs," O'Connor tells us, "with the grand self-confidence of a mountain . . . surveying everything." Yet from her proud promi-nence Mrs. Shortley is destined to fall with sudden and spec-tacular finality, visited by Judgment so complete, a displacement so total, "she seemed to contemplate for the first time the tremendous frontiers of her true country".[44]

The story, moreover, is a superb example of the use of the freak in literature, his deployment as an image of our own

[44] See her first collection of stories, *A Good Man Is Hard to Find* (New York: Farrar, Straus and Giroux, 1955). See also her essay "The Fiction Writer and His Country", which concludes with the following passage from Saint Cyril of Jerusalem, which adorned that collection: "The dragon sits by the side of the road, watching those who pass. Beware lest he devour you. We go to the Father of Souls, but it is necessary to pass by the dragon." Her commentary on this text is beautiful and incisive: "No matter what form the dragon may take, it is of this mysterious passage past him, or into his jaws, that stories of any depth will always be con-cerned to tell, and this being the case, it requires considerable courage at any time, in any country, not to turn away from the storyteller." O'Connor, *Mystery and Manners*, p. 35.

displacement: from grace, God, the purposes of ideal being, all that conduce to draw men home to Heaven. Every character in the story, excepting the old priest and the peacocks, is a freak, leaving the sensitive reader to savor the most exquisite irony of all, namely, that those who least regard themselves as such, Mrs. Shortley, for example, provide in fact the most appalling specimens of freakishness. "She thrashed forward and backward, clutching at everything she could get her hands on and hugging it to herself . . . then all at once her fierce expression faded into a look of astonishment and her grip on what she had loosened." It is the moment of Judgment, swift and terrible; and there is simply no escaping its terrible resolution, in the direction of which everything in that story moves with an almost Sophoclean sense of doom. One is brought to the realization, finally, that everyone has been displaced—by others, yes—but most important of all, by sin, and suffering, and Death. Yet it is only by means of such displacement that the characters might, in the end, need God enough to see him for the first time.

"There is a moment in every great story", O'Connor writes, "in which the presence of grace can be felt as it waits to be accepted or rejected." The average reader might not recognize the moment, she adds, lacking the "sharp eye for the almost imperceptible intrusions of grace", but his insensibility very much needs to be overcome. Even violence may not be enough to awaken the reader to the encounter. Still, the writer has got to try. In her own stories, O'Connor writes, "I have found that violence is strangely capable of returning my characters to reality and preparing them to accept their moment of grace. Their heads are so hard that almost nothing else will do the work. This idea, that reality is something to which we must be returned at considerable cost, is one which is seldom understood by the casual reader, but it is one which is implicit in the

Christian view of the world." And she reminds us that violence, while never an end in itself, is always a force to be used for good or evil, something by which we are told the Kingdom of Heaven may be taken.[45]

One thinks at once of the Misfit in "A Good Man Is Hard to Find", the lead story in O'Connor's first collection, who, in shooting the silly old grandmother on the last page, delivers a Judgment whose violence enables her at last to accept *her* moment of grace. " 'She would of been a good woman,' the Misfit said, 'if it had been somebody there to shoot her every minute of her life.' " Or the story called "Revelation" (from O'Connor's final collection, *Everything That Rises Must Converge*), which presents an ordeal of Judgment so searing that the character on whom it is inflicted must undergo a veritable rebirth in order to endure it. Poor Mrs. Turpin, who thought herself impregnably superior to very nearly the whole human race, is about to have a revelation the nature of which will pulverize the structures of her universe. She too appears at first larger than the life around her. (The opening scene is a doctor's waiting room, and Mrs. Turpin, "who was very large, made it look even smaller by her presence . . . looming at the head of the magazine table . . . a living demonstration that the room was inadequate and ridiculous".) O'Connor describes Mrs. Turpin as having "little bright black eyes", which she uses to draw mostly invidious comparisons with other people, fixing their lesser status in the universe she orders.

> Sometimes at night when she couldn't go to sleep, Mrs. Turpin would occupy herself with the question of who she would have chosen to be if she couldn't have been herself. If Jesus had said to her before he made her, "There's only two places available

---

[45] See her essay "On Her Own Work", in *Mystery and Manners*, pp. 107–18.

for you. You can either be a nigger or white-trash," what would she have said? "Please, Jesus, please," she would have said, "just let me wait until there's another place available," and He would have said, "No, you have to go right now and I have only those two places so make up your mind." She would have wiggled and squirmed and begged and pleaded but it would have been no use and finally she would have said, "All right, make me a nigger then—but that don't mean a trashy one." And He would have made her a neat clean respectable Negro woman, herself but black.

Yes, it is all so very neatly set out, these secure structures of Mrs. Turpin's tidy little self-serving universe; only the premises must never be disturbed. How often, too, it moves her to protestations of false humility, to an ersatz gratitude offered up to a wise Providence with sense enough not to have unduly inconvenienced her standing in the social order. "Her heart rose. He had not made her a nigger or white-trash or ugly! He had made her herself and given her a little of everything. Jesus, thank you! she said. Thank you thank you thank you! Whenever she counted her blessings she felt as buoyant as if she weighed one hundred and twenty-five pounds instead of one hundred and eighty."

It will all come to grief soon enough: violent, unforgettable disaster awaits Mrs. Turpin in the very room she had entered so commandingly a few moments before. It comes in the form of a demented Wellesley College student, a total stranger, hurling a huge book, hilariously called *Human Development,* square in the eye of her unsuspecting target. She thereupon leaps across the table, howling, her fingers seeking the soft flesh of Mrs. Turpin's throat. A short struggle ensues. The lunatic girl is subdued, but not before pronouncing sentence. "Mrs. Turpin's head cleared and her power of motion returned. She leaned forward until she was looking directly into the fierce brilliant eyes. There was no doubt in her mind that the girl did know her, knew her in some intense and personal way, beyond time and place and condition. 'What you got to say to me?' she asked hoarsely and held her breath, waiting, as for a revelation."

It comes with the force of divine Judgment itself: "The girl raised her head. Her gaze locked with Mrs. Turpin's. 'Go back to Hell where you came from, you old wart hog,' she whispered. Her voice was low but clear. Her eyes burned for a moment as if she saw with pleasure that her message had struck its target."

However, it is only in the aftermath of the attack, the period during which Mrs. Turpin struggles vainly to make sense of, to wrest meaning from, the event, that the exact nature of her encounter with this second of the Four Last Things will be shown. " 'I am not,' she said tearfully, 'a wart hog. From Hell.' But the denial had no force. The girl's eyes and her words, even the tone of her voice, low but clear, directed only to her, brooked no repudiation. She had been singled out for the message, though there was trash in the room to whom it might justly have been applied." By day's end, in the course of a titanic struggle with God himself (" 'How am I a hog?' she demanded. 'Exactly how am I like them? . . . There was plenty of trash there. It didn't have to be me' "), she will come to the realization lying at the very heart of mystery. Bent over the pig parlor, gazing at her own hogs—who appear, says O'Connor, "to pant with a secret life"—she is at last vouchsafed the vision that heretofore had eluded her. Lifting her head to see a purple streak across the sky, a numinous light erupts to reveal the certain knowledge God wishes her to take to her death:

> She saw the streak as a vast swinging bridge extending upward from the earth through a field of living fire. Upon it a vast horde of souls were rumbling toward Heaven. There were

whole companies of white-trash, clean for the first time in their lives, and bands of black niggers in white robes, and battalions of freaks and lunatics shouting and clapping and leaping like frogs. And bringing up the end of the procession was a tribe of people whom she recognized at once as those who, like herself and Claud, had always had a little of everything and the God-given wit to use it right. She leaned forward to observe them closer. They were marching behind the others with great dignity, accountable as they had always been for good order and common sense and respectable behaviour. They alone were on key. Yet she could see by their shocked and altered faces that even their virtues were being burned away. She lowered her hands and gripped the rail of the hog pen, her eyes small but fixed unblinkingly on what lay ahead. In a moment the vision faded but she remained where she was, immobile.

. . . In the woods around her the invisible cricket choruses had struck up, but what she heard were the voices of the souls climbing upward into the starry field and shouting hallelujah.[46]

Now the Church of course traditionally speaks of Judgment in two ways, both the Particular, or Proximate, Judgment, of which poor Mrs. Turpin's vision is a fiery and clear foretaste, and the Final, or General, Judgment, which awaits all mankind at the end of the world. It is a useful distinction the Church draws here. Certainly it is necessary and fitting that the soul, in all its unique particularity of life and history, be made to

---

[46] It is the final passage from a story that ends on a note of utter apocalyptic triumph. Of course, given the cauterizing nature of her vision, it may take Mrs. Turpin a while longer before she's quite ready to assimilate the joy. But that she eventually would, O'Connor had no doubt whatsoever. "You got to be a very big woman to shout at the Lord across a hogpen", she wrote in a letter. "She's a country female Jacob. And that vision is purgatorial." The story, by the way, was written in the last year of O'Connor's life, and it won the O. Henry award for best fiction when it was published. O'Connor died in August of 1964.

confront itself in that blinding moment of awareness before God that immediately follows upon the death of the body. How else can it finally know the true weight of its worth in God's eyes unless he show it at once and unmistakably to each created existence? To put off that realization until the General Judgment at the end of history would leave the soul in unnecessary suspense about its ultimate fate. "And while the friends were still standing in tears by the bedside the soul of the sinner was judged", writes Joyce in the *Portrait of the Artist as a Young Man.* "At the last moment of consciousness the whole earthly life passed before the vision of the soul and, ere it had time to reflect, the body had died and the soul stood terrified before the judgment seat."[47]

What else, then, is the Particular Judgment if not an encounter with the living God, before whom all the dross of a man's life is consumed in the fire of divine Judgment, leaving only that which is truly lasting. Each of us will then know himself exactly as he is known, without any possibility of error regarding the meaning of his life. The soul will see how God judges, and conscience will confirm the justice of the sentence; yes, even if a man must rise up and renounce his very self. "For those who die in mortal sin, estranged from God, it will be a confirmation of all the horror of death itself. For others it will be the very beginning of their victory over the death they have just experienced."[48]

On what basis, then, can there be Judgment if not because man is free, therefore responsible before the One who gave him life and liberty in the first place? There has got to be this

---

[47] From *The Essential James Joyce,* edited by Harry Levin (London, England: Jonathan Cape, 1948), p. 138.

[48] See James T. O'Connor, *Land of the Living: A Theology of the Last Things* (New York: Catholic Book Publishing, 1992), p. 105.

final reckoning of the use—and abuse—man has made of his freedom, of the talents given him by God to bring to perfection before eternity itself. The crucial decision for each of us, then, is to render that final Yes to God that makes the gift of his mercy efficacious. "By rejecting grace in this life," the *Catechism* teaches, "one already judges oneself, receives according to one's works, and can even condemn oneself for all eternity by rejecting the Spirit of love."[49]

Nevertheless, there remains as well a Final Judgment awaiting all of us. This will necessarily be definitive and universal and will take place following the general resurrection of the body at the end of the world, whose promised union with the soul and their joint disposition for all eternity will then be determined before all men by God. No one knows the day or the hour, when the Son of God shall come; it is reserved to the Father alone to fix the time.[50] But with the coming of Christ in triumph at the end of time all men will rise with their bodies to

[49] CCC, 679.

[50] CCC, 1040. See also Romano Guardini, *The End of the Modern World,* the final passage of which reads, "I proclaim no facile apocalyptic. No man has the right to say that the End is here, for Christ Himself has declared that only the Father knows the day and the hour (Matthew XXIV, 36). If we speak here of the nearness of the End, we do not mean nearness in the sense of time but nearness as it pertains to the essence of the End, for in essence man's existence is now nearing an absolute decision. Each and every consequence of that decision bears within it the greatest potentiality and the most extreme danger." Guardini's disclaimer is especially helpful of course as we approach the end of the second millennium, a time in which the temptation to spin scenarios of the "facile apocalyptic" appear to be everywhere. His profound and prophetic book was written in the aftermath of the destruction of Nazi Germany, intended as a search for orientation amid the ruins of the modern age. It was first published in this country by Henry Regnery Company in 1956 with an introduction of haunting eloquence by Frederick Wilhelmsen.

give a complete account of all that they ever did or failed to do. "Then will the conduct of each one and the secrets of hearts be brought to light. Then will the culpable unbelief that counted the offer of God's grace as nothing be condemned."[51] Only then will the Son pronounce his final word on the meaning of all being. "We shall know the ultimate meaning of the whole work of creation and of the entire economy of salvation and understand the marvelous ways by which His Providence led everything towards its final end."[52]

This Final Judgment must ineluctably be public, a social event, as it were, since it will demonstrate in the most apodictic and unmistakable fashion the terms of God's justice and mercy. Indeed, it will unfailingly manifest to all who ever lived both the justice of God in condemning sinners and the depth of his mercy to those who are saved. The General Judgment, then, is an event destined to take place in the presence of the glorified Christ, amid all the resurrected bodies at the very end of the world. And in that blazing Presence that is Christ, who is Truth itself, and to whom all Judgment has been given by the Father in virtue of his redeeming work on the Cross,[53] every man who has ever lived will stand, the truth of whose relationship to God having been laid completely bare before the world. "The last Judgment will reveal even to its furthest consequences the good each person has done or failed to do during his earthly life."[54] Truth will at last vanquish all that stands against it, making finally and forever clear that "if God exists, truth must be the absolutely last word".[55]

[51] CCC, 678.
[52] CCC, 1040.
[53] CCC, 679.
[54] CCC, 1039.
[55] See Reginald Garrigou-Lagrange, *Life Everlasting: A Treatise on the Four Last Things* (Rockford, IL: Tan Books, 1952), p. 82.

Hell

The life of man is one of ceaseless toil and unrelenting struggle, lived out amid circumstances that, in the end, conspire to kill him. Time being a sort of unforgiving river of ephemeral events, and none more fleeting than the man who knows his fate, no sooner does the current bring one life into view than another is swept clean away. As Saint Gregory the Great writes, "Man cometh forth like a flower from concealment, and of a sudden shows himself in open day, and in a moment is by death withdrawn from open view into concealment again. The greenness of the flesh exhibits us to view, but the dryness of dust withdraws us from men's eyes."[1]

From green shoot to gray dust: how brief is man's estate in this world. Yesterday the womb, tomorrow the tomb. And so little laughter and joy in between. "Round and round the fire" the life of man revolves, writes Eliot in his moving and lyric evocation of the English country folk of East Coker, their immemorial lives moving to the rhythms of a rustic mortality:

> Earth feet, loam feet, lifted in country mirth
> Mirth of those long since under earth
> Nourishing the corn . . .

[1] From his work *Morals on the Book of Job.* Quoted in *Death: A Book of Preparation and Consolation,* selected by Barry Ulanov (New York: Sheed and Ward, 1959), p. 11.

> The time of the seasons and the constellations
> The time of milking and the time of harvest
> The time of the coupling of man and woman
> And that of beasts. Feet rising and falling.
> Eating and drinking. Dung and death.[2]

Note how the rhythmic rise and fall of their lives evokes the same patterned ebb and flow of human life recorded in the great Wisdom literature of the Old Testament; in Ecclesiastes, for example, there is this well-known verse: "All things have their season, and in their times all things pass under Heaven. A time to be born and a time to die. A time to plant, and a time to pluck up that which is planted. A time to kill, and a time to heal. A time to destroy, a time to build. A time to weep, and a time to laugh. A time to mourn, and a time to dance. . . . A time to keep, and a time to cast away."[3] Eliot, in reproducing something of these inspired cadences of Israelite poetry, rediscovers a kindred sense of time, of so many disparate stones gathered and scattered, which mark the village life of his East Coker ancestors.

But all this undulating movement of life, the patterned dance of human living, the felt shiver of men who live under sentence of death, will of course change the moment this frail flower we call life is rudely plucked and tossed away. There on the cusp of eternity—"The undiscover'd country", Shakespeare calls it, "from whose bourn / No traveller returns"[4]—the lot of man will no longer be subject to time's ravages; rather will

---

[2] From *Four Quartets,* the second movement of which is "East Coker".

[3] Qo 3:1–6.

[4] See Shakespeare's *Hamlet,* act III, sc. 1, where the brooding prince ponders "the dread of something after death", which stays the hand of the would-be suicide.

his destiny be to go on and on forever. All the choices we have made along the way, tending for good or evil as we move inexorably toward death, all that will carry us to one or another everlasting end. Only one of two possibilities ultimately looms for man, toward either of which destination one is moving from moment to moment, and those are Hell or Heaven.

Surely no two words summon more powerfully the latent and dramatic possibilities of being human. The image of the one conjuring all that is most deeply embedded in human desire and longing: joy, freedom, peace, delight, perfection, God. The other an image of sorrows unspeakable, compact of all that we most dread and abhor: infernal solitude, enmity, evil, ennui. If life is a battleground fought out between God and the Devil in which all the resources of Heaven and Hell are loosed, then man is the prize to be won or lost by either side. "Everything nudges our elbow", writes Tom Howard.

> Heaven and Hell seem to lurk under every bush. The sarcastic lift of an eyebrow carries the seed of murder, since it bespeaks my wish to diminish someone else's existence. To open a door for a man carrying luggage recalls the Cross, since it is a small case in point of putting the other person first. We live in the middle of all of this, but it is so routine that it is hard to stay alive to it. The prophets and poets have to pluck our sleeves or knock us on the head now and again, not to tell us anything new but simply to hail us with what has been there all along.[5]

As ol' Huck Finn puts it in Mark Twain's classic American coming-of-age tale, "I was a-trembling because I'd got to decide forever betwixt two things, and I knowed it. I studied for a

---

[5] See his comprehensive study *The Novels of Charles Williams* (San Francisco: Ignatius Press, 1991), p. 18.

minute, sort of holding my breath, and then says to myself, 'All right, then, I'll go to Hell.' "[6]

If Heaven be the state of blessed exchange—I to another and all to the Eternal Other—then Hell bespeaks that which is always opposite, to wit, a condition of total and quite terrifying solitude and silence, where the damned shall be left alone forever. Gomorrah is the term Charles Williams used to describe that ultimate choice of self.

> If Heaven is the real city, then Sodom, where they reject real, fruitful exchange for a barren and sterile parody, is a sort of reverse city; and, in Williams' scheme, Gomorrah is yet one remove further away, the place of final silence and solitude. . . . An air, not only of evil, but more, of remoteness and silence and impenetrable loneliness, hangs over Gomorrah, since we know nothing about it at all.[7]

In short, Hell is the place, call it a condition or state of soul, where God cannot be found, nor can he find us; where all the reassuring lights of faith and hope and love have gone out. "If there is damnation", muses the narrator of A. Dubos' short story "Rose",

> and a place for the damned, it must be a quiet place, where spirits turn away from each other and stand in solitude and gaze haplessly at eternity. For it must be crowded with the passive: those people whose presence in life was a paradox; . . . (who) witnessed evil and lifted neither an arm nor a voice to stop it, as they witnessed joy and neither sang nor clapped their hands.[8]

[6] See his *Adventures of Huckleberry Finn,* chap. 31.

[7] Howard, *Novels of Charles Williams,* pp. 259–60.

[8] A. Dubos, *The Last Worthless Evening* (Boston: Godine, 1968), p. 194. There are three kinds of people, it has been proverbially remarked: those who make things happen, those who watch things happen, and those who wonder what happened. Of these, the latter surely go to Hell, the sheer weight of their indifference drawing them gravitationally down into doom.

But who nowadays even believes in Hell, much less the prospect of actually going there? Our age is awash in sentimentalism and man, who imagines himself altogether innocent of evil (every man his own Immaculate Conception!), is often tempted to think himself meant for an afterlife of effortless and unending bliss. That is, when he thinks of an afterlife at all, which is fairly infrequent given the impacted fallout from secularism, whose noxious fumes have choked so much of the atmosphere of the past four hundred years. "The confiscation of the spiritual riches of Christianity by men who no longer believe in Christianity" is how Denis de Rougmont memorably put it, striking the necessary parasitic note that so aptly describes the pathology.

In a totally secularized world, whither the claims of eschatology? Alas, they reduce to irrelevancy for all those who, in Dietrich Bonhoeffer's unfortunate phrase, have "come of age".[9] Nowadays we look after ourselves and thus have no need to call upon the quaint, antediluvian gods to remedy our condition. Modern society, with its vaunted material prosperity, its militant and pervasive secularity, exhibits an almost Faustian impatience with limits; bent on keeping even Death at bay, it evinces scant interest in the continued maintenance of Hell, surely the least palatable of all the Christian doctrines proposed for our belief. Yet, at no time in her two-thousand-year history has the Church not affirmed either the existence of Hell or the eternity of the torments awaiting those who choose to go there. What, then, is the truth about Hell, which, despite the obvious howls of modern disapproval, the Church persists in teaching? And has it anything to commend to our lives?

The first and most obvious point it would seem useful to make about Hell is that if it does not exist then Christ, who so

9 Cited by Martin C. D'Arcy, *Humanism and Christianity,* (New York and Cleveland: World Publishing, 1969), p. 2.

clearly and frequently refers to it in the pages of holy Scripture, is a liar. For example, in the justly famous chapter of Saint Matthew where Jesus gives his listeners the Beatitudes, quite hair-raising references are made to Hell, to the fire and the damnation awaiting those who neglect or disdain their observance. The Sermon on the Mount, for all that uninformed opinion would have us believe, is not all sweetness and light. "And if your right hand causes you to sin, cut it off and throw it away; it is better that you lose one of your members than that your whole body go to Hell."[10] What is the sentimentalist Christian to do with statements like this? Is he to cut it off and throw it away lest it give scandal to his heart? Or this: "And do not fear those who kill the body but cannot kill the soul; rather fear him who can destroy both soul and body in Hell."[11] If Jesus had taken such pains to warn us away from Hell, it can only be that it must exist and that some of us may yet be in peril of going there.

Thus Jesus not only brandishes the most menacing threats imaginable against sinners in this life (whole cities as well: "And you, Capernaum, will you be exalted to Heaven? You shall be brought down to Hell"[12]), he also seems most fearfully explicit about the details of the Judgment to come, the ordeal to which our sins will have brought us face to face. Addressing those on his left at the very last, he will say to them, "Depart from Me, you accursed, into the eternal fire prepared for the devil and his angels; for I was hungry and you gave Me no food, I was thirsty and you gave Me no drink, I was a stranger and you did not welcome Me, naked and you did not clothe Me, sick and in prison and you did not visit

10 Mt 5:30.
11 Mt 11:28.
12 Mt 11:23.

Me."[13] Of course they will bleat and wail in wonderment at Christ's disguising himself behind the hungry and thirsty, those sick or in prison; and he will answer them with the finality of thunder, "Truly, I say to you, as you did it not to one of the least of these, you did it not to Me."[14] And the sinners, damned by their own admission, will fall away into eternal punishment, while the righteous will be swept up into eternal life.

All that Jesus says on the subject of Hell would appear then to have but one purpose, to persuade man of its existence and of the real possibility that at the end of his life he may take himself there. Concerning Hell and all its attendant horrors, there can be no quibbling, no attempt to blunt the intolerable edge of the truth. The only sin, Chesterton says, is to call green grass gray. And the cleverest ruse of the devil is to try and persuade man that neither he nor Hell exists. The stratagem has proven itself strikingly successful in our age, when disbelief about the Old Guy has reached virtual epidemic levels. As Msgr. Ronald Knox used to say, it is so stupid of the twentieth century to have abandoned belief in the devil when he is the only explanation for it. In any case, as Joseph Ratzinger remarks, "the idea of eternal damnation, which had taken ever clearer shape in the Judaism of the century or two before Christ, has a firm place in the teaching of Jesus, as well as in the apostolic writings. Dogma takes its stand on solid ground when it speaks of the existence of Hell and of the eternity of its punishments."[15] If the Founder of the Christian religion would not scruple to keep silent about Hell, that is, if God himself testifies to both

[13] Mt 25:41–43.

[14] Mt 25:45.

[15] Joseph Ratzinger, *Eschatology—Death and Eternal Life* (Washington, D.C.: Catholic University Press, 1988), p. 215.

the certainty of the fact and the fear we ought all entertain lest we fall into it, then it is hardly the Church's business to stand mute before the reality now.

Besides, doesn't the fact itself certify in the most clear and unmistakable way that man is free, that the exercise of his liberty is not make believe, not an instance of that whimsicality in which, like children dressing up to be different, man plays at being the free, swashbuckling agent of the moral life? Surely the Pope is right when, framing the question in that way, he asks, "Is not hell in a certain sense the ultimate safeguard of man's moral conscience?"[16] How otherwise can man expect his freedom to be respected if God will not honor his right to throw it away? And himself as well? A human liberty that does not include the right to say No to God, yes, even to the point of rejecting his summons to love forever, is no liberty at all. Here we touch upon one of the deepest mysteries of man, namely, his freedom to sever the profoundest and most intimate metaphysical link of all, that of existence itself. One could almost define man as a being free to break the umbilical cord with Being, to burn his last bridge to God. Man alone possesses a liberty so radical that it can choose its own annihilation. Animals, as far as we know, are not candidates for despair. Eliot, in an acute psychological study of the French poet Baudelaire, puts it in a way that has never been improved upon:

---

[16] See his *Crossing the Threshold of Hope* (New York: Knopf, 1994), p. 186. The Pope speaks here of the mystery, "truly inscrutable, which embraces the holiness of God and the conscience of man", whereby no man is authorized to judge another, to consign his soul to everlasting torment. "The silence of the Church is, therefore, the only appropriate position for Christian faith. Even when Jesus says of Judas, the traitor, 'It would be better for that man if he had never been born' (Mt 26:24), His words do not allude for certain to eternal damnation."

So far as we are human, what we do must be either evil or good; so far as we do evil or good, we are human; and it is better, in a paradoxical way, to do evil than to do nothing: at least, we exist. It is true to say that the glory of man is his capacity for salvation; it is also true to say that his glory is his capacity for damnation. The worst that can be said of most of our malefactors, from statesmen to thieves, is that they are not men enough to be damned. Baudelaire was man enough for damnation: whether he is damned is, of course, another question, and we are not prevented from praying for his repose. In all his humiliating traffic with other beings, he walked secure in this high vocation, that he was capable of a damnation denied to the politicians and the newspaper editors of Paris.[17]

Certainly the *Catechism of the Catholic Church,* in which the connection between human liberty in this life and eternal perdition in the next is plainly drawn, would agree: "Mortal sin is a radical possibility of human freedom.... If it is not redeemed by repentance and God's forgiveness, it causes exclusion from Christ's kingdom and the eternal death of hell, for our freedom has the power to make choices for ever, with no turning back."[18] In short, it is wrong so to trivialize man's dignity that in this most awesome discharge of human freedom, in which the soul decides for or against God forever, the full seriousness of what may be undertaken is treated as mere child's play.

In every life, however brief its duration, the essential drama of existence unfolds against an absolute horizon beckoning man to one or another eternal possibility. In the course of each

[17] See his essay on Baudelaire in *Selected Prose of T. S. Eliot,* edited with an introduction by Frank Kermode (New York: Harcourt Brace Jovanovich, 1975), p. 236. The essay was first published in 1930.

[18] CCC, 1861.

man living out the allotted portion given him by God, he finds himself poised between hope of the one and fear of the other. This is a good and salutary thing. It is not well to be without both a lively hope of getting to Heaven, which is the heart's deepest longing, and holy fear lest we get Hell instead, which will consist of a final sundering of man from God, the utmost catastrophe ever to threaten man, alongside of which even planetary disasters pale into insignificance. On that basis, Josef Pieper is clearly onto something when he writes that one must assume

> that something is not quite in order when a man is afraid of nothing, and that the ideal of "stoic" invulnerability and fear-lessness is based on a false interpretation of man and of reality itself.
>
> Thomas Aquinas points, in particular, to three passages of Holy Scripture, which, incidentally, are scarcely known to contemporary Christianity, as proof that fearlessness as a funda-mental attitude—which, in any event can "be maintained" only through self-deception—is nothing short of unnatural. Accord-ing to Thomas, the first passage, which is from the book of Job, refers to fearlessness that has its source in a presumptuous pride of mind: " ... He was made to fear no one" (Job 41:24); the second passage is from Sirach: " ... He that is without fear cannot be justified ... " (Sir 1:28); the third is from the book of Proverbs: "A wise man feareth and declineth from evil" (Prov 14:16).[19]

And why is that? Because, again, there can be no worse disaster to befall man than sin, whose wages are Death and Hell. "It is to the fearfulness of this very real possibility," notes Pieper, "which is always rising anew from the ground of the creature's being—to the fearfulness of being separated by sin

[19] Josef Pieper, *On Hope* (San Francisco: Ignatius Press, 1986), pp. 78–79.

from the Ultimate Ground of all being—that the fear of the Lord, which is a true fearfulness, affords the only true answer."[20] Which fear, it needs constant emphasizing, is among the Gifts of the Holy Spirit, the conferring of which is central to the whole rite of Confirmation.

Inasmuch as both the beginning and end of all things remain hidden from us (after all, it is only the actual living that falls in between, in parentheses as it were, that we know), no man may surmise the outcome of his life, the verdict of *his* particular trial. I simply do not know that I shall go to Heaven, and I ought therefore to fear the prospect that I may not escape going to Hell. Certainly I may hope, indeed, I am obliged to do so, that God and his grace will be sufficient for me to persevere to the end and thus avert the worst. But I do not know this. "From this perspective," observes Balthasar,

> we can understand the splendid statement by Kierkegaard: "I have never been so far in my life, and am never likely to get farther than to the point of 'fear and trembling', where I find it literally quite certain that every other person will easily be blessed—only I will not. To say to the others: you are eternally lost—that I cannot do. For me, the situation remains constantly this: all the others will be blessed, that is certain enough—only with me may there be difficulties."[21]

The only wisdom we can hope to acquire, says Eliot, is the wisdom of humility: "Humility is endless."[22]

---

[20] Ibid., p. 81.

[21] Hans Urs von Balthasar, *Dare We Hope "That All Men Be Saved"?* (San Francisco: Ignatius Press, 1988), p. 88.

[22] From "East Coker", *Four Quartets.* Near the end Eliot reminds us of that which only humility can secure: "There is only the fight to recover what has been lost / And found and lost again and again: and now under conditions / That seem unpropitious. But perhaps neither gain nor loss. / For us, there is only the trying. The rest is not our business."

We only know that we do not know, which leaves us to hope for all that we cannot yet know. What else is hope if not our willingness, in the teeth of all that appears desperate, to transcend the empirically given situation and thus to throw ourselves trustingly upon God? In hope we ground all that we have and are in Christ, the very One in whom, to quote the Preface of the Mass for the Dead, "has dawned for us the hope of a blessed resurrection, heartening with a promise of immortality to come to those of us who are saddened by the certainty of dying". Fearful, too, of the prospect of the Second Death, an eternity of unquenchable fire, of never seeing the Blessed Face of God.

It is this fact, by the way, that determines man's essential status as pilgrim, wayfarer, a creature in transit, bound to one or another unending destination. Along the way, indeed, at every turn in the road, we are free to succumb to one or another form of hopelessness; to flirt with either, however, will push us dangerously close to the edge, over which lies Hell. The first is Presumption, which is a fairly serious sin whose malice consists in our attempting to lay hold of Heaven in advance of God offering it to us. Insofar as we *think* we have actually obtained Heaven, we relax our grip on hope itself, its basic tension now giving way to the sudden certainty of its possession. Saint Augustine, in fact, calls it a perverse security (*perversa securitas*), consisting of a duplicitous dependence on that for which there is no warrant. Pieper calls it "a perverse anticipation of the fulfillment of hope".[23] However, the other and far more lethal variant is that of despair, which is the absence of any hope at all, "a perverse anticipation of the

---

[23] See chap. 4 of Pieper, *On Hope,* which meticulously unpacks the sin of presumption, pp. 65–73.

nonfulfillment of hope", says Pieper.[24] Both are damnable offenses that, if unrepented, will carry their subjects straight to Hell.

Among the casualties these two enemies of salvation inflict is of course the whole life of prayer, which the spiritual masters tell us is indispensable to hope; particularly petitionary prayer, that is, the Our Father, which is grounded in hope. What else is prayer but the voicing of our hope? As Pieper writes, "One who despairs does not petition because he assumes that his prayer will not be granted. One who is presumptuous petitions, indeed, but his petition is not genuine because he fully anticipates its fulfillment."[25]

Nevertheless, in judging the proportion of iniquity between the two, the lesser sin is surely that of presumption. The reason for this goes right to the heart of who God is, in the real distinction between the immanent and economic Trinity and the metaphysical primacy given to being over against doing. Aquinas, not surprisingly, has drawn the necessary distinction: "Because of his infinite goodness, it is more proper to God to spare and to show mercy than to punish. For the former belongs to him by reason of his nature, the latter only by reason of our sins."[26] To expect mercy from one who is shot through and through with mercy ("I will make good all that is defective", Christ tells Julian of Norwich.[27] Or this from a Christmas play written by Saint Thérèse of Lisieux: "I myself am

[24] Ibid., p. 47.
[25] Ibid., p. 70.
[26] Quoted in ibid., p. 71. "In other words," says Pieper, "the anticipation of fulfillment is not so contrary to man's real existential situation as is the anticipation of nonfulfillment. The ungrounded certainty of presumption is less contrary to human nature than is despair."
[27] See Balthasar, *Dare We Hope,* pp. 101–2.

the Judge of the world, and my name is Jesus"[28]) is surely not so unreasonable a conviction as the utter certainty of one who despairs of God's willingness to deliver him from Hell.

"Do not presume", says Augustine, "one of the thieves was lost. Do not despair: one of the thieves was saved." It is of course the latter that proves most lethal. Here is the radical, relentless posture of one who literally insists on never "giving a damn". Such an attitude of mind, forever fixated upon itself, is essentially an invitation to be damned. "In Dostoevsky's novel *The Brothers Karamazov* Father Zossima says: 'Fathers and teachers, I ponder 'What is hell?' I maintain that it is the suffering of being unable to love. Once in infinite existence, immeasurable in time and space, a spiritual creature was given, on his coming to earth, the power of saying, 'I am and I love.' "[29]

Not to exercise this capacity for love, to refuse concretely to love another (especially the poor and the unloved), anchoring all one's *eros* to self alone: this is the philosophy on which Hell depends. And, to be sure, God, taking us finally at our word — again, that terrifying compliment paid to creatures on whom, from the very start, the liberty to despise felicity had been conferred — will not stop us. We are not, after all, infants shorn of responsibility for the use we make of our freedom. If Heaven reposes upon God's grace and our freedom, so too must Hell. "The specificity of Christianity is shown in this conviction of the greatness of man", writes Ratzinger. "Human life is fully serious. . . . The irrevocable takes place, and that includes, then, irrevocable destruction."[30] Indeed, he reminds

[28] Ibid., p. 105.
[29] Cited by Pieper in *About Love,* in *Faith, Hope, Love* (San Francisco: Ignatius Press, 1997), p. 228.
[30] Ratzinger, *Eschatology,* pp. 217–18.

us, it is a seriousness so acute that it was given definitive form in the Cross of Christ. And so we remain breathtakingly free right to the end, at liberty therefore to declare before God, in words that echo throughout Lewis' sublime allegory *The Great Divorce,* "Not Thy will, but mine be done." And so it is done, forever. Under the weight of an impacted, infernal solipsism the soul ineluctably sinks into everlasting doom. "There was a door", cries the loveless, self-tormenting husband to his unloving wife in Eliot's *Cocktail Party,*

> And I could not open it. I could not touch
> the handle.
> Why could I not walk out of my prison?
> What is Hell? Hell is oneself,
> Hell is alone, the other figures in it,
> Merely projections. There is nothing to escape from
> And nothing to escape to. One is always alone.[31]

True enough, each of us creates his own Hell; the heart of man, says Sir Thomas Browne, is that place where the devils do most dwell. "I feel sometimes a Hell within myself."[32] It is an ancient and recurrent theme. In the *Aeneid,* for example, Virgil reminds us how "each man bears his own Hell."[33] Or Christopher Marlowe, embroidering upon the Faustus motif, a great and enduring staple of Western literature, has the character Lucifer exclaim:

---

[31] T. S. Eliot, *The Cocktail Party: A Comedy* (London: Faber and Faber, 1949), p. 87.

[32] See his *Religio Medici* (1642), pt. I, sec. 51.

[33] See Virgil's *Aeneid,* bk. VI, l. 743. Also Milton, *Paradise Lost,* bk. I, l. 253:

Why this is Hell, nor am I out of it;
Think'st thou that I who saw the face
    of God,
And tasted the eternal joys of Heaven,
Am not tormented with ten thousand
    Hells,
In being deprived of everlasting bliss?

Hell hath no limits, nor is circumscribed
In one self place; for where we are is
    Hell
And where Hell is there must we ever be.[34]

Or C. S. Lewis, in our own time, making the identical
point about Hell, to wit, "Every shutting up of the creature
within the dungeon of its own mind—is, in the end, Hell."[35]

It is, therefore, the soul of insolent dishonor to impute
responsibility to God for it. Despite Dante's inscription above
the portals of Hell,[36] despite the exquisite literary detail fur-
nished by James Joyce, whose *Portrait of the Artist as a Young*

A mind not to be chang'd by place or
    time.
The mind is its own place, and in itself.
Can make a heav'n of hell, a hell of
    heav'n.

34 See his *The Tragical History of Doctor Faustus* (1604).
35 Lewis, *The Great Divorce* (New York: Macmillan, 1946), p. 69.

36   I AM THE WAY INTO THE CITY OF WOE.
        I AM THE WAY TO A FORSAKEN PEOPLE.
        I AM THE WAY INTO ETERNAL SORROW.

        SACRED JUSTICE MOVED MY ARCHITECT,
        I WAS RAISED HERE BY DIVINE OMNIPOTENCE,
        PRIMORDIAL LOVE AND ULTIMATE INTELLECT.

Man is filled with harrowing features of hellish landscape,[37] it is not God who fashioned that final state of self-imposed exile and torment we call Hell. It is surely not out of an outraged justice that the sufferings of the damned are wrought. The unquenchable fire about which so many Scripture texts speak is not set by God, his wrath igniting the wood of an eternal conflagration. In the unreal world of Joyce's novel, for example, one encounters a mad Jesuit Retreat Master, whose specialty, one gathers, is to sermonize at endless and sadistic length a class of hapless young boys, their minds filled with the most lurid nonsense about Hell, all of whose torments issue forth from a tyrant God literally delighting in torturing the bodies and souls of unrepentant sinners. "And through the several torments of the senses the immortal soul is tortured eternally in its very essence amid the leagues upon leagues of glowing fires kindled in the abyss by the offended majesty of the Omnipotent God and fanned into everlasting and ever-increasing fury by the breath of the anger of the Godhead."[38] And on and on it goes, the fury of an enraged Jehovah stretched to quite sickening lengths. Alas, it is a fairly typical Joycean

---

Only those elements time cannot wear
Were made before me, and beyond time I stand
Abandon all hope ye who enter here.

See canto III, Dante's *Inferno,* translated by John Ciardi.

37 See especially pp. 134–48. From *The Essential James Joyce.*

38 "The damned howl and scream at one another, their torture and rage intensified by the presence of beings tortured and raging like themselves. All sense of humility is forgotten. The yells of the suffering sinners fill the remotest corners of the vast abyss. The mouths of the damned are full of blasphemies against God and of hatred for their fellow sufferers and of curses against those souls which were their accomplices in sin" (p. 146).

effusion. Of course, the trouble with Joyce, as someone once waggishly put it, is that he never got beyond the First Week of the Ignatian Exercises, with their remorselessly serious and necessary examination of the pains of Hell, which sinners do most emphatically stand in peril of facing if they persist in their wrongdoing. But to suggest that God is even remotely responsible for the hellish sufferings with which the Exercises threaten the obdurate is simply grotesque. It is both untrue to being and ungenerous to God. Hell is not *his* creation. Rather, Hell, and the fires therein, are lit entirely from within by the flames of sin that men and angels commit against the order of divine love. "The only hope, or else despair", writes Eliot in a sublimely penetrating passage from his *Four Quartets,*

> Lies in the choice of pyre or pyre —
> To be redeemed from fire by fire.

"Who then devised the torment?" he asks in the following stanza.

> Love is the unfamiliar Name
> Behind the hands that wove
> The intolerable shirt of flame
> Which human power cannot remove.
> We only live, only suspire
> Consumed by either fire or fire.[39]

The implication is plain, however infelicitously put when rendered in prose: man is meant to endure either the fire of God, the Holy Spirit, whose flaming Pentecostal descent inspires the soul with the love of God and neighbor; or else the hellish and devouring fire of the self-centered self, fed by the accumulated sins of pride, avarice, lust, anger, and the rest, which set

[39] See the last of his *Four Quartets,* "Little Gidding".

the soul to blaze forever with the torment of its own self-willed rejection of God. We are not thrown by Another into the sea of fire; it is our own sins that fill that sea, each a seething cauldron of self-imposed enmity and pain. "At a certain point," writes Origen, the great Church Father of the early third century,

> in a soul that has accumulated all sorts of evil deeds and sins, this mixture catches fire and begins, in punishment of the soul, to burn. If, through God's power, the spirit will have before its eyes the history of all the offenses committed by it in shame and godlessness, then its conscience will be stung by its own barbs; it will be its own accuser and witness. Just as the violent separation of our limbs and the dislocation of the joints of our body cause enormous pains, so the soul that finds itself outside of the order and harmony for which it was created by God will itself suffer the pain and punishment of its transgressions and inconstancies and disobedience.[40]

How far from the precincts of orthodoxy we have fallen between the time of Origen and James Joyce! Under the circumstances, the least permissible thing for Christians to do is to flirt with any assignation of guilt or responsibility to God for the hellishness of the choices his creatures make. In a very moving passage that Balthasar quotes from Gustave Martelet, S.J., the following formulation is given, which, unlike the sadism attributed to God by Joyce's imaginary Jesuit, genuinely endeavors to present the real truth about God and Hell found in the New Testament.

Insisting that the nature of final damnation be seen in the light of that overpowering divine love, which the creature is yet free to forfeit and lose, Martelet writes,

[40] *Peri Archon* II, 10:4–5, slightly abbreviated. Cited in Balthasar, *Dare We Hope,* pp. 51–52.

Certainly there is talk of fire, worm and the second death that
excludes one from the kingdom.... But hell, as refusal of
divine love, always exists on one side only: on the side of him
who persists in creating it for himself. It is, however, impossible
that God himself could cooperate in the slightest way in this
aberration, above all, not for the purpose of vindicating the
magnificence of his denied love through the triumph of his
righteousness, as has, unfortunately, often enough been claimed.
Thus, if there is any reaction in God to the existence of hell—
and how could there not be such a reaction?—then it is one of
pain, not of ratification; God would, so to speak, find a brand
burned into his flesh: we can guess that it has the form of the
Cross. Our pain in the face of hell would then be only an echo
of his own pain. The meaning of the New Testament text is
thus surely not, "Hear of what is to befall you" but rather
"Hear of what should in no case befall you". If Christ speaks to
us in the Gospel of the possibility of man's becoming lost
through a refusal of love, then certainly this is not in order that
it should happen, but only in order that it should not happen.
How could Christ, who has thrown himself against death and
sin, impose such a loss, even consent to it, given that he has,
after all, done everything to avoid it?[41]

Two questions remain to be answered about Hell: one, the
exact nature of its pains, and two, the number of those
condemned to suffer them. As regards the first, the teaching of
the Church set out in the *Catechism* is very clear: there is
chiefly the pain of loss, which amounts to an eternal separation
from God, "in whom alone man can have the life and happiness
for which he was created and for which he longs".[42] Without
question, to be deprived of the sight of God, the pleasure of his
company for all eternity, must be the most horrifyingly acute

41 Ibid., pp. 54–55, n. 10.
42 CCC, 1057.

pain of all. Think of it: the loss of the very sight of God, a countenance no more gracious than which can be imagined! To stand at last before that face of the living God, only to hear the words, *I do not know you. Depart from me. Go to a place of your own.* To hear that dolorous dismissal reecho throughout endless corridors of that place that our sins have made compact forever. It is a prospect so dismaying, so calculated to dizzy and appall, that nothing in this world exists to equal the horror of it. In the New Testament we are solemnly told that if we love God and keep his Commandments, then we in turn will be known and loved by him—forever. A very strange promise, indeed, but of its fulfillment there can be none greater, none more profoundly sought. In the end nothing matters more to man than that God, his Creator and Redeemer, should deign to recognize and approve him. To love and thus to shine his countenance upon him forever. It is nothing less than the weight of divine glory itself. And to those left bereft of that by their sin, what possible loss could be greater than this? "I know that many tremble at the mere mention of Gehenna," writes Saint John Chrysostom,

> but for me the loss of this higher glory is more terrible than the tortures of hell. A thousand hells would be nothing in comparison with the loss of this magnificence that is meant to make us eternally blessed: what torment to be one from whom Christ turns away, to have to hear from his mouth: I do not know you, to be accused by him of not having given him food when he was hungry.[43]

There is also of course the pain of sense, the suffering of the body that, while not to be understood in a merely physical way, that is, sadistic tortures, is nevertheless not purely spiritual either, particularly not in light of the Last Judgment, when

---

[43] Quoted in Balthasar, *Dare We Hope,* p. 50.

the bodies of the lost will share in the punishment of their souls. Lewis, in a trenchant passage,[44] reminds us how in the New Testament Christ uses three symbols to convey the idea of Hell, of that state of ultimate pain and forlornness to which the damned are driven by the obduracy of their sins. To begin with, Hell has got to be understood as a place of punishment, "everlasting punishment", Christ calls it in Matthew 25. Secondly, it is spoken of as a place of destruction, which accounts for the repeated warning that we are only to "fear him who is able to destroy both body and soul in Hell". And, finally, of course, Christ speaks of it as a place of final privation, exclusion, or banishment into "the darkness outside", as in the mysterious parables of the man without his wedding garment and the foolish virgins who without oil for their lamps must go out to meet the waiting Bridegroom.[45]

As for fire, which we are right sensibly to fear, something of Hell's ineffable torment and destruction is certainly suggested by the recurrent use of this image. The Church, with full scriptural warrant, speaks of fire, but the image aims to capture a reality profoundly deep, as witness the following text from Isaiah: "The light of Israel will become a fire, and his Holy One a flame; and it will burn and devour his thorns and briers in one day."[46] Reflecting on this text, the German bishops write,

> Just as heaven is God himself, won for ever, so hell is God himself eternally lost. The essence of hell is *final exclusion from communion with God* because of one's own fault. Because God alone is fulfillment of man's meaning, the loss of God in hell brings the experience and the pain of ultimate meaninglessness and despair.[47]

[44] See Lewis' chapter on Hell in *The Problem of Pain,* pp. 118–28.
[45] Ibid., p. 124.
[46] Is 10:17.
[47] See *The Church's Confession of Faith: A Catholic Catechism for Adults* (San Francisco: Ignatius Press, 1987), p. 347.

Again, not to see God on the other side, save for that instant of Judgment when under the weight of the self-accusing self one sinks into the lake of fire, must itself be a suffering of the most consuming sort. And while it is not necessary to draw upon sulphurous images of burning brimstone that rages on and on with unspeakable and unending intensity, one is nonetheless constrained to admit that, unless we are to dismiss all of Scripture as a tissue of lies, the integrity of the Church's doctrine requires that among the myriad horrors of Hell provision must be made also to include this mysterious pain of sense.

In summarizing the position of the New Testament, C. S. Lewis puts it very well, I think. "You will remember," he comments, recalling the image of Matthew 25:

> the saved go to a place prepared for them, while the damned go to a place never made for men at all. To enter Heaven is to become more human than you ever succeeded in being in earth: to enter Hell, is to be banished from humanity. What is cast (or casts itself) into Hell is not a man: it is "remains". To be a complete man means to have the passions obedient to the will and the will offered to God: to have been a man—to be an ex-man or "damned ghost"—would presumably mean to consist of a will utterly centred in its self and passions, utterly uncontrolled by the will. It is, of course, impossible to imagine what the consciousness of such a creature—already a loose congeries of mutually antagonistic sins rather than a sinner— would be like.[48]

A couple of images come to mind that may help to crystallize the idea. In the movie *La Strada,* which came out many

[48] Lewis, *Problem of Pain* (New York: Macmillan, 1972), pp. 125–26. The remainder of this chapter, following this citation from Lewis, has been excerpted from Regis Martin, *The Suffering of Love: Christ's Descent into the Hell of Human Hopelessness* (Petersham, Mass.: St. Bede's Publications, 1995). These excerpts are used with permission.

years ago, there is a character named Zampano, the circus strongman played with riveting pathos by Anthony Quinn, whom we see at the very end, broken and alone on a deserted beach, his fists pounding the sand as he remembers the dead, dim-witted girl with whom he once lived, whose simple dreams he had brutally smashed. She had only wanted someone to love, and he had answered her with impacted ferocity: "I don't need anyone. I want to be left alone." He had gone on to murder her one friend, the circus fool, who alone of all the circus performers had given her a reason to hope, to believe that the world was good and decent and had need even of her. All that Zampano had destroyed in his willful and terrible betrayal and desertion of her, leaving her soul prey to the torments of a final loneliness. But then the whole harrowing realization of all that he has done and lost in a lifetime's treachery, a life of perfidy so profound it touches the depths of Hell, suddenly illumines the face of this ravaged man at the last, and the viewer is overwhelmed by the sight. "Never are we less protected against suffering than when we love", writes Freud, whom Pieper quotes approvingly in his study *About Love.* [49] Who can doubt but that Zampano, in the midst of his heart-wrenching loss, is experiencing for the first time man's genuine need for another, his unwillingness indefinitely to be left alone. "Love anything," Lewis assures us, "and your heart will certainly be broken. If you want to make sure of keeping it intact, you must give your heart to no one, not even to an animal."[50] Even Zampano, for all his brutishness, is no animal; he too hungers for that love that, in order to receive, you must first give recklessly away to another. Failing that test of love's true mettle, he flails haplessly away at the sand in desperate, damnable sorrow.

[49] Cited by Pieper in *Faith, Hope, Love*, p. 228.
[50] Ibid., p. 76.

A second image is drawn from a short story by Flannery O'Connor called "The Artificial Nigger", one of the deepest things she ever wrote,[51] in which an old man and his grandson journey into the dark city, where the boy undergoes an unspeakable ordeal of abandonment at the hands of his own grandfather. The latter, in considering what he had done to his own flesh and blood, undergoes himself a searing experience of shame and loss, of a loneliness whose proportions must be very near to what the pain of eternal loss means to those condemned everlastingly to Hell. And although certain distinctions need to be observed (for instance, that the old man's sin is even now, within the story's own rhythm of loss and gain, being expiated, and that there is time in which to expiate it), notwithstanding all that, before genuine forgiveness can begin the sinner must know something of what O'Connor has called the depth of his denial. This depth awaits exploration, and, in fact, to the degree that its depths are plumbed, so too the soul's correlative ascent.

This particular sinner, in any case, is forced to feel the full depth of his denial in the most salutary way; the story thus is a dramatization of sin and suffering and grace to redeem. He experiences a state of abandonment, of sheer estrangement and enmity from the one living relation God had given him to love, which thrusts him out into a world of such privation and loss as to be, *mutatis mutandis,* indistinguishable from Hell. O'Connor's description is worth quoting in full, for it is frightfully lucid:

> When Mr. Head realized this [realized, that is, what he had done and the child's refusal to forgive what he had done] he lost all hope. His face in the waning afternoon light looked

51 Flannery O'Connor, from *A Good Man Is Hard to Find* (New York: Farrar, Straus and Giroux, 1995).

ravaged and abandoned. . . . He knew that now he was wander-
ing into a black strange place where nothing like it had ever
been before, a long old age without respect and an end that
would be welcome because it would be the end. . . . He felt he
knew now what time would be like without seasons and what
heat would be like without light and what man would be like
without salvation.

Finally, there is the image of the selfish giant (the story is
told by Oscar Wilde),[52] whose garden is perpetually bleak
and wintry because he has never allowed himself to love
another. But one morning he awakens to the loveliest of sounds
(it is only a linnet, but so starved has the giant been for love
that its music lifts his soul); rushing to his window, he sees a
little boy out in the garden struggling to climb onto the
branches of a tree. At once the giant's heart melts as he looks
out. "How selfish I have been!" he says. "Now I know why the
Spring would not come here. I will put that poor little boy on
the top of the tree, and then I will knock down the wall, and
my garden shall be the children's playground for ever and ever."

So he steals quietly behind the boy, lest the sight of him
distress the child, and gently places him high up into its branches,
which immediately burst into blossom. The little boy thereupon kisses the giant, at the sight of which all the other
children return excitedly into the garden. There they play for
many years, though the mysterious little boy never returns,
and when asked the others confess that they have never seen
him.

One day, however, when the giant has grown very old, he
observes the child once more in his garden and goes out to him

[52] "The Selfish Giant", in *The Complete Fairy Tales of Oscar Wilde*
(New York: Franklin Watts, 1960).

in joy and gladness. But on seeing the child, his face suddenly grows red with anger and alarm, and he says, "Who hath dared to wound thee?" For on the palms of the child's hands were the prints of two nails, and the prints of two nails were on the little feet.

> "Who hath dared to wound thee?" cried the Giant. "Tell me, that I may take my big sword and slay him."
>
> "Nay," answered the child: "but these are the wounds of Love."
>
> "Who art thou?" said the Giant, and a strange awe fell on him, and he knelt before the little child.
>
> And the child smiled on the Giant, and said to him, "You let me play once in your garden; today you shall come with me to my garden, which is Paradise."
>
> And when the children ran into the garden that afternoon, they found the Giant lying dead under the tree, all covered with white blossoms.

What if there really were a loneliness so complete and final that nothing in this world could remedy the sorrow of it? A state of abandonment so definitive that neither word nor gesture could deliver us from it? Would not that frightful condition find its precise and formal theological equivalent in what we call Hell? Isn't Hell that very depth of loneliness where no love, no relation of real communion, can reach one in order to set free the soul of one's solitude? A life bereft of both hope and home, lacking all sense of community, or sanctuary, or escape? The Prodigal Son fated never to find his father's love but, like the Flying Dutchman, left aimless and alone forever—an eternity of grief, no less... who could endure it?

In her memoir of short story writer John Cheever, his daughter Susan explains the origin of the book's title, *Home*

Before Dark, which includes the following moving vignette on the theme of what life would be like were any of us, at the last, unable to get home before dark:

> My father liked to tell a story about my younger brother Fred.... Once, at twilight after a long summer day, my father was standing outside the house under the big elm tree that shaded the flagstones in front of the door. Fred came back from playing with some friends, worn out and tired too, and when he saw Daddy standing there he ran across the grass and threw his little boy's body into his father's arms.
>
> "I want to go home, Daddy," he said, "I want to go home." Of course he was home, just a few feet from the front door, in fact. But that didn't make any difference, as my father well understood. We all want to go home, he would say when he told this story. We all do.[53]

And what if there were no home to go to, no one to welcome the child when he got there (when it comes to going home we are all children); indeed, our own father telling us in words so final that nothing more will ever be said to soften the sentence, "I do not know you"?

Finally, as regards (for some anyway) the tantalizing prospect of knowing who in fact is in Hell, writhing amid exquisite fires of unending torment, the Church has no information whatsoever and, indeed, is forbidden even to speculate. Neither the number of the lost nor the names of any whom we might imagine to be lost have ever been revealed. It is simply not part of the sacred deposit of faith, the public Revelation that ended with the death of the last apostle. Nor is it seemly to inquire. Augustine spent an entire book detailing the punishments, condign or otherwise, to be meted out to the denizens of Hell, pursuant to his darkly pessimistic vision of *massa*

---

[53] Susan Cheever, *Home Before Dark: A Biographical Memoir of John Cheever* (Boston: Houghton Mifflin, 1984), pp. 10–11.

damnata, but he dared not put names beside any of them.[54] It is given to no man the knowledge of any man's outcome. Augustine cannot know that Hell is filled with the godless, nor can Origen know that it is empty, all the godless having repented and gone to Heaven. We can be certain of neither Judas Iscariot's damnation nor that of Adolph Hitler, to cite two villains of history. However infamous the chronicles of wicked men, it is not for other men, still less for Christ's Church, to pronounce on their eternal destiny. The Church has raised up many but may pronounce as reprobate none. And all the Church's strictures on the subject are meant to remind the faithful of the following constant, namely, that the distinct possibility exists that it is *I* who may go to Hell, not my neighbor or any of the countless rogues and rascals who swell the annals of human depravity. Thus we are free to hope, to trust in God's mercy that it may yet, in the language of the letter of Saint James, "triumph over justice".[55]

Let the Church's *Catechism* provide the last word on the subject, sufficient therefore to slake the curiosity of those who ask the question: "God predestines no one to go to hell; for this, a willful turning away from God (a mortal sin) is necessary, and persistence in it until the end."[56] Who then can look into a man's soul at the last (who, indeed, dares to look at any time, peering with prurient interest into the heart of another), to presume to judge the worth of all that he has brought before God? Only God, we are told, who has given us no list of names, only the knowledge that Hell and eternal damnation are possible, that we need fear them, especially we, his putative friends, who so often are in danger of betraying him.

54 See his *City of God,* bk. XXI, chap. 18.

55 "For judgment is without mercy to one who has shown no mercy; yet mercy triumphs over justice" (James 2:13).

56 CCC, 1037.

Heaven

There was once a learned and resourceful professor of theology, armed with many degrees, who delivered a long and tedious lecture on Heaven, the very Last Thing ever to be remembered. Excessively painful and pedantic as it was, however, the ordeal ended with the learned professor's happy disclaimer that, of course, nothing he had said on the subject was to be confused with the thing itself. Heaven, he confessed brightly, is certain to be infinitely more delightful than anything he might laboriously work up in attempting to throw light on Man's Last End.

The point is, we had better keep our pretensions, however scholarly, strictly modest. Indeed, anyone pronouncing on the subject of Heaven is open to the charge of being an impostor inasmuch as all of us are presuming to say something about that which we know nothing. None of us has been there, nor have we ever spoken to anyone who has. What silver-tongued speaker exists whose words can compare to an experience literally beyond words? Can mere daughters of the earth, to use Dr. Johnson's image, match the splendor and sublimity of the sons of Heaven?[1]

[1] See the introduction to his massive dictionary, in which mere words are assigned an earthly status while the things to which they point are given the exalted status of Heaven.

The figure of Lazarus, who lay dead for days before the Lord brought him back, doubtless had seen something of that World beyond the Wardrobe, to borrow a line from Lewis' tantalizing *Chronicles of Narnia,* but what news did he bring back? "What difference did his journey into eternity make to him?" asks Gerald Vann at the beginning of *The Divine Pity.* "How did it alter his way of life when he returned to the world of time?" All we are told, Vann reminds us, is that at a subsequent supper in Bethany at which Jesus sat at table, Lazarus was one of those reclining at the table. "You imagine the practical, motherly Martha having to tell him repeatedly at mealtimes: 'Lazarus, do get on with your food.' "[2]

Could the bemused man have possibly been thinking of something else? Perhaps a more celestial cuisine was on his mind. And who, for that matter, can imagine an eternity without supper? Certainly not the Fathers at the Second Vatican Council, who say of all human goods, that in Heaven "we will find them once again, cleansed this time from the stain of sin, illuminated and transfigured".[3] Like the fellow in the Flannery O'Connor story, whose hunger for Heaven, she says, "was so great that he could have eaten all the loaves and fishes after they were multiplied".[4] We should all look forward with the keenest pleasure to that Banquet on the other side. Nothing less than the most vast and sumptuous feast, we are told, awaits those who long for the Bread of Life.[5]

[2] Gerald Vann, O.P., *The Divine Pity: A Study in the Social Implications of the Beatitudes* (1945; reprint, Glasgow: William Collins Sons, 1977), p. 7.

[3] See *Gaudium et Spes,* no. 39.

[4] The reference is to Tarwater, a fierce and prophetic figure drawn from the imagination of O'Connor, who moves through her final novel, *The Violent Bear It Away* (New York: Farrar, Straus and Giroux, 1960). The passage is on the penultimate page of the book.

[5] Those who hunger for bread are not to be given stones, Jesus assures us in the Gospels. For a wonderful and charming foreshadowing,

But what exactly are we to make of Heaven? This last and Final Thing in God's inventory—What is it, and where are we to find it? Certainly for great numbers of self-styled enlightened folk, as straightjacketed by modernity as any lunatic in an asylum, Heaven is the ultimate taboo, the breaking of which is simply not to be borne. Not unlike the effort to ban tobacco and guns, which our secular elites think so worthy an endeavor, interest in the afterlife is adjudged dangerous and atavistic, a species of benightedness against which the omnicompetent state must needs inoculate its citizens. Some years ago, Hollywood, that egregious taste maker of modern man, actually breached the outer ramparts in a movie called *The Rapture,* in which a born-again mother, journeying into the desert fastness, there to await the End, shoots her daughter in the head when God, clearly having a different schedule in mind, fails to beam the faithful remnant back home to Glory. A movie of spectacular silliness, *The Rapture,* for all its apocalyptic flirtatiousness, is even worse than *Heaven Can Wait,* which heretofore had struck the usual showbiz note on eschatology.

In other words, no one really knows much of anything about Heaven. As John Donne once put it in a splendid

---

see the short story by Isak Dinesen, "Babette's Feast", since made into an extraordinary film, which powerfully conveys something of the rich sacramentality of the Catholic Eucharist and the promised Paradise it contains. It tells the story of two perfectly dour Danish sisters of rigid piety, not to mention insipid diet, into whose lives steps a mysterious Parisian cook, whose climactic gift of an inconceivably sumptuous supper furnishes an analogue of Heaven and the ineffable mercy of God. The story ends when one of the sisters, her plate scarcely put away after the Feast, exclaims to Babette, whose savings were all dissipated by the lavishness of this one dinner, " 'Yet this is not the end! I feel, Babette, that this is not the end. In Paradise you will be the great artist that God meant you to be! Ah!' she added, the tears streaming down her cheeks. 'Ah, how you will enchant the angels!' " Taken from *Anecdotes of Destiny and Ehrengard* (New York: Vintage Books, 1993), p. 59.

sermon on the subject, in which even he, the dazzling word-smith of Saint Paul's (whose myriad and erudite effusions on the sacred text once moved James I, his Dread Sovereign, to announce that Master Donne, like God himself, "surpasseth all understanding"), positively shrank from the attempt to mount an exegesis of the meaning of that highest and holiest thing:

> He that asks me what Heaven is, means not to hear me, but to silence; he knows I cannot tell him: when I meet him there, I shall be able to tell him, and then he will be as able to tell me; yet then we shall be able to tell one another, this, that we enjoy is Heaven, but the tongues of angels, the tongues of glorified saints, shall not be able to express what that Heaven is; for even in Heaven our faculties shall be finite.[6]

So the effort to fit an infinite experience into a finite mind, like the proverbial circle that cannot be squared, necessarily resists even the most prodigious of created intellects. In relation to the place where God dwells amid the ineffable splendors of his own household, we are all very much like the wretched young schoolboy whom C. S. Lewis describes in *The Weight of Glory,* to wit, forced to labor pathetically over details of grammar and syntax while the joys of poetry remain a sadly unconsummated delight. "The Christian," writes Lewis,

> in relation to Heaven, is in very much the same position as this schoolboy. Those who have attained everlasting life in the vision of God doubtless know very well that it is no mere bribe, but the very consummation of their earthly discipleship; but we who have not yet attained it cannot know this.... [P]oetry replaces grammar, gospel replaces law, longing transforms obedience, as gradually as the tide lifts a grounded ship.[7]

[6] Sermon XXIII.

[7] C. S. Lewis, *The Weight of Glory and Other Addresses* (reprint, Grand Rapids: Wm. B. Eerdmans, 1979), p. 3.

In other words, compared to the experience of the pleasures that actually await us in Paradise, we are all reduced to a sort of gibbering, palsied inadequacy of speech the moment we try and describe them. As the *Catechism of the Catholic Church* reminds us, the whole mystery of Heaven, of communion with God in Christ, and therefore with each other, simply beggars all understanding. "Scripture speaks of it in images: life, light, peace, wedding feast, wine of the kingdom, the Father's house, the heavenly Jerusalem, paradise: 'no eye has seen, nor ear heard, nor the heart of man conceived, what God has prepared for those who love him.' "[8]

Nevertheless, to steal a line from Chesterton, if a thing is worth doing at all, then it is worth doing ill. Next to the job of actually getting into Heaven, which is a work of grace, one might argue that the effort to write about Heaven is important, too, if only as a work of nature. And does not nature too pine for Paradise? After all, in all the creeds of Christendom, especially those of most ancient and apostolic usage, the Church refers to God as "Creator of Heaven *and* earth". He alone is architect and preserver of all that is, whether seen or unseen. The God who ushers the universe into being is also the One who graciously fashions an abode of perfect blessedness where his angels and saints dwell in rapturous delight with the God-head forever. God is thus understood, according to the Church's profession of faith, as author of both Cosmos and Covenant, of Nature and Grace. In the circumstance, man becomes benefici-ary of a double blessing, of being both given and forgiven by the selfsame God. Given in the order of nature, of existence, and then, all creation having come to grief in sin, graced by the encounter with Christ in forgiveness, in the unimaginable order of salvation that confers Heaven: "the ultimate end and

[8] CCC, 1027.

fulfillment of the deepest human longings, the state of supreme, definitive happiness".[9]

The Church has always made much of this point, this nexus struck by a wise and loving Providence between human nature and divine grace, seeing in it "the bond, deep within creation, that both unites heaven and earth and distinguishes the one from the other".[10] Earth, then, is man's place, the state in which sin and death engulf and destroy him; while Heaven remains God's own place, the nature of which places it beyond time and space, beyond the realm where sin and suffering abound. "Heaven consists in such a relationship with God", observes Frank Sheed, "that no created nature, by its own powers, could be adequate to it."[11]

Yet, in light of this whole mysterious nature/grace dynamic—that is, "the paradox of the spiritual creature that is ordained beyond itself by the innermost reality of its nature to a goal that is unreachable for it and that can only be given as a gift of grace"[12]—it can only be to this precise place and condition that man has been called. The result of that very God-shaped vacuum that Augustine and other Church Fathers intuited at the heart of man, a divinely hollowed-out space only Christ could fill. How many glints of that heavenly glory have already fallen into this world, cascading down from the celestial heights in order to awaken, to stir into life, that essential hunger for God, for the "Father's house".[13] That place to which we have

9 CCC, 1024.

10 CCC, 326.

11 Frank Sheed, *A Map of Life: A Simple Study of the Catholic Faith* (reprint, San Francisco: Ignatius Press, 1994), p. 34.

12 Hans Urs von Balthasar, *The Theology of Henri de Lubac* (San Francisco: Ignatius Press, 1991), p. 13.

13 Jn 14:2.

all been summoned simply in virtue of God having first called us into existence. The mysterious election in Christ before even the world was made, an election that the blood of his Cross would seal forever. "Look Lord," says the poet Donne, "and find both Adams met in me; / As the first Adam's sweat surrounds my face, / May the second Adam's blood my soul embrace."[14]

Man is thus a creature made for God, called into being so that he might receive and answer yet another call, one intended to draw him definitively home to God. Here we confront the deepest datum of all, namely, man's single indestructible ardor for God, for an eternity spent in the most intimate, blessed communion with him. "Heaven is our fatherland, and there is our true home", writes Fr. Gleason, S.J. "Its essential splendor is that eternal vision of God, face-to-face, which is itself the beatifying source of our endless happiness."[15]

How profoundly humanity needs eternity! All hope short of Heaven is simply too short. And, to be sure, it is only eternity that can give time itself validity before God. "If a person's death is worthless," observes Ratzinger,

> then his life is worthless too. If man is ultimately jettisoned in death, if he becomes as so much refuse, then he is, even beforehand, one of the things that humanity can jettison and

[14] John Donne, "Hymn to God My God, in My Sickness", in *The Complete Poetry and Selected Prose of John Donne,* ed. Charles M. Coffin (New York: Random House, 1952), pp. 271–72.

[15] Robert W. Gleason, S.J., *The World to Come* (New York: Sheed and Ward, 1958), p. 147. Today, as Joseph Ratzinger reminds us, "we are all well aware that the word 'Heaven' does not designate a place beyond the stars but something much greater and more difficult to express, namely, that God has a place for us and that God gives us eternity." See his *Co-Workers of the Truth: Meditations for Every Day of the Year* (San Francisco: Ignatius Press, 1992), p. 376.

can treat as such. But if man never becomes refuse, if his value is called eternity, then this value is always his and marks his whole life. . . . Only eternity can unite present and future. It always transcends the moment, is always more than we presently have, but it is not limited just to the future, it always extends even now into all our days. Those who have talked us out of our belief in heaven, or would like to talk us out of it, have not given us the earth in exchange but have made it desolate and empty, have covered it with darkness. We must find once more the courage to believe in eternal life with all our heart.[16]

Surely it is this longing and desire for God, for that Heaven he alone confers, that most profoundly defines the whole human project. A seething, unappeasable *eros* amid the many ridiculous idolatries that man in his flagrant forgetfulness of God cannot completely uproot from his mind and heart! "You have made us for yourself, O God, and our hearts remain ever restless until they find rest in You", as Augustine memorably puts it at the beginning of his *Confessions*.[17]

Or, again, to cite those marvelous and exquisite lines from *The City of God,* where Augustine gives stirring expression of what the joys of Heaven will finally consist: "There we shall rest and we shall see; we shall see and we shall love; we shall love and we shall praise. Behold what shall be in the end and shall not end."[18]

What a splendid time we shall have, an eternity no less of rest and sight, of love and praise. We remain conscious, therefore, of a desire and longing for that which no human and earthly happiness can provide, a place of infinite and perfect repose, which simply does not exist in this world. However gorgeous

---

[16] Ratzinger, *Co-Workers of the Truth,* p. 356.
[17] See bk. I, chap. 1.
[18] See his *The City of God,* bk. XXII, chap. 30.

the sunsets, or ardent and deep the friendships, nothing in this world will finally satisfy. Awaken and arouse, yes, but never to allay this perpetual longing for God, who mysteriously plants this desire deep within the soul of every created being.

This perfect life with God—in which, to recall the *de fide* teaching of Benedict XII, the blessed "see the divine essence with an intuitive vision, and even face to face, without the mediation of any creature"—this certainly is Heaven.[19] We shall become like God himself, so the Scriptures tell us, because we shall see him as he is. Our soul will thus be riveted upon God forever. Whether as supreme truth, as the Dominicans taught, which means our intellect will never come to an end of seeing him, or as supreme goodness, as the Franciscans held, which means our will will never come to an end of loving him, is really no great matter of dispute. In the last analysis, says Ratzinger, "the point of it all is the same: God totally permeates the whole man with His plenitude and his utter openness. God is 'all in all,' and thus the human person enters upon his boundless fulfillment."[20] Or, as the inimitable Chesterton once put it, "Whether the supreme ecstasy is more affectional than intellectual is no very deadly matter of quarrel among men who believe it is both, but do not profess even to imagine the actual experience of either."[21]

Thus, declares Henri de Lubac in his great, seminal work *The Mystery of the Supernatural*,

> The desire to see God cannot be permanently frustrated without an essential suffering . . . for is not this, in effect, the defini-

[19] Quoted in CCC, 1023.

[20] Ratzinger, *Eschatology—Death and Eternal Life* (Washington, D.C.: Catholic University Press, 1988), p. 235.

[21] See E. L. Mascall, *Grace and Glory* (Denville, N.J.: Dimension Books, 1961), p. 64.

tion of the "pain of the damned"? ... And consequently—at least in appearance—a good and just God could hardly frustrate me, unless I, through my own fault, turn away from Him by choice. The infinite importance of the desire implanted in me by my Creator is what constitutes the infinite importance of the drama of human existence.... My finality, which is expressed by this desire, is inscribed upon my very being as it has been put into this universe by God. And, by God's will, I now have no other genuine end ... except that of "seeing God".[22]

We have all been called home to Heaven, to that very "province of Joy" to which the Archangel Raphael summons all pilgrims; "whose home", writes Ernest Hello in a sublime prayer composed in honor of this great saint of happy meetings, who once led the blind Tobias to where he needed to be, "lies beyond the region of thunder, in a land that is always peaceful, always serene and bright with the resplendent glory of God".[23]

And yet, concerning this, which Lewis, in his "Weight of Glory" sermon, has called "our own far off country"—toward which even now we may surprise in ourselves a certain stirring— one is nevertheless constrained by a certain shyness. One almost, he says, commits an indecency in speaking of it. "I am trying to rip open the inconsolable secret", which we all possess but whose pain is such that we take our "revenge on it by calling it names like Nostalgia and Romanticism and Adolescence", the secret, he says, so sweetly piercing that the mere mention of it awakens that awkwardness we commonly associate with first love.[24]

[22] Henri de Lubac, *The Mystery of the Supernatural,* translated by Rosemary Sheed (New York: Herder and Herder, 1967), p. 70.

[23] See Flannery O'Connor, *The Habit of Being,* edited and with an introduction by Sally Fitzgerald (New York: Farrar, Straus and Giroux, 1979), pp. 592–93. It was a prayer she said every day for many years.

[24] Lewis, *Weight of Glory,* p. 4.

Only more, of course ... infinitely, surpassingly more. Because it is finally here that we locate that ultimate and highest thing of all, on which faith and hope remain forever fixed.

In short, it is God himself whom we seek and in whose presence we are promised sure and perfect delight. For God, as Saint Thomas reminds us, "by the very fact that He exists, is truth. Therefore the intellect that sees God cannot but rejoice in the vision of Him." Who, moreover—Aquinas continues—"is goodness itself, and goodness is the cause of love.... Consequently, in the vision of God, Who is goodness and truth itself, there must be love or joyous fruition, no less than comprehension. This accords with Isaiah 66:14: 'You shall see and your heart shall rejoice.' "[25]

It may well be, as George Macdonald reminds the young visionary who finds himself mysteriously on board the bus bound for glory in Lewis' *Great Divorce,* an enthralling entertainment in which free weekend passes are offered the inmates of Hell to tour the outer precincts of Heaven (if they like the place, they are encouraged to stay; most, however, return as disgruntled and rebellious as when they set out). It may well be, as Macdonald says, that "Hell is a state of mind" and that "every state of mind, left to itself, every shutting up of the creature within the dungeon of its own mind—is, in the end, Hell. But Heaven is not a state of mind. Heaven is reality itself. All that is fully real is Heavenly."[26]

Indeed, all the way to Heaven is Heaven, to recall the words of Christ spoken to Saint Catherine of Siena, because "I am the Way." Surely this fact is what accounts for the tremendous solidity of the place, its perfect, eternal palpability, and not

[25] St. Thomas Aquinas, *Compendium Theologiae,* p. 165.
[26] Lewis, *The Great Divorce* (New York: Macmillan, 1946), p. 65.

that imagined ethereality so enamored of by the Platonists of every age. Evidence of this can be found throughout Lewis' story. For example, the young man, moved by a sudden impulse, bends down to pluck the merest flower growing at his feet, to wit, a single divine daisy, but it neither breaks nor bends. "I tugged till the sweat stood out on my forehead and I had lost most of the skin off my hands", he says.[27]

Another example involves the Episcopal Ghost, who despite every appeal to reason and grace—what his Eminence is pleased to call "crude salvationism"—will obstinately persist in refusing what alone and infallibly confers ultimate happiness and do so practically on the front porch of Paradise! Consider the sheer perverse hilarity of this thoroughly dead and dishonest bishop, droning endlessly on about his "little Theological Society" in Hell, whose membership he aims to instruct on "what a different Christianity we might have had if only the Founder had reached His full stature [that is, had not gone to Golgotha] . . . how this deepens the significance of the Crucifixion. One feels for the first time what a disaster it was: what a tragic waste . . . so much promise cut short."[28]

Heaven, says Macdonald, in concluding the case against so preposterous an exercise in Episcopal solipsism, Heaven is not a place of sterile debate, "for I will bring you to the land not of questions but of answers, and you shall see the face of God".[29] A face, alas, too real and terrible for the bishop to bear, which is why, returning on the same bus that brought him, he will remain self-condemned forever, reading fussy little theology tomes of endless, infernal futility. As Dorothy Sayers once remarked about the condition of damnation, it is "without

[27] Ibid., p. 19.
[28] Ibid., p. 40.
[29] Ibid., p. 36.

direction or purpose . . . nothing to do and all eternity to do it in".[30]

What then is Heaven but that place where a man may savor freely the taste of truth, whose flavor is like honey and whose embrace that of the Bridegroom? There, a man's thirst may be quenched forever.

"I shall know the fullness of joy, when I see your face, O Lord . . . fulfillment and endless peace in your presence", to cite the evening prayer of the Church. Or, to draw upon the rich hymnographic traditions of the Church, so much of it resonant with truth mere discourse cannot equal, there is this final stanza from the text of a nineteenth-century hymn translated from the Spanish by Christian Henry Bateman: "On heaven's joyful shore His goodness we'll adore, singing forevermore, 'Alleluia! Amen!' "

In other words, the whole ensemble of future unending glory is here laid out: an eternity of repose and vision, of love and worship in the company of God himself. Here is the supreme, final end of man, this direct unmediated vision of God, whom to behold is perfect, inexhaustible joy and bliss. "The regions where there is only life", says Macdonald, "and therefore all that is not music is silence."[31]

Music and silence and not, Heaven knows, the cacophonous noise of Led Zeppelin, Janis Joplin, or the Beach Boys but rather the music of the immortal Wolfgang Amadeus Mozart, in the purity of whose sound one glimpses the triumphal forms of ultimate transcendent joy. Hell is for rock music and all its satanic seductions. But for the angelic spheres, where all sound and silence alternate in that perfected praise of being, there is

---

[30] Quoted by Mascall in *Grace and Glory,* pp. 23–24.
[31] Ibid., p. 24.

room only for Mozart, and Bach, and Beethoven . . . and perhaps a moment or two of purified jazz, my colleague Mark Miravalle on the sax. As Joseph Ratzinger tells us, "When the word becomes music, there is . . . a perceptible taking on of flesh . . . a drawing upon the hidden resonance of creation, a discovery of the song which lies at the basis of all things."[32]

Meanwhile, of course, we find ourselves somehow stuck in the body, not in a gnostic sense, surely, but nevertheless steeped in bodies full of weight and extension, in transit between time and eternity, moving toward yet another Monday morning. In other words, in this vale of tears we are often enough tempted to feelings of entrapment, and thus the task of soul making, of shaping ourselves for that eventual moment of final elevation into eternity, really does necessitate eyes trained on hope, on Heaven, beseeching God in the spirit of Eliot's "Ash Wednesday", to

> Teach us to care and not to care
> Teach us to sit still
> Even among these rocks,
> Our peace in His Will
> And even among these rocks
> Sister, mother
> And spirit of the river,
> Spirit of the sea,
> Suffer me not to be separated
>
> And let my cry come unto Thee.[33]

Here, to be sure, is the universal note of all Christian hope and striving, struck again and again in the voices of all the

---

[32] Joseph Ratzinger, Address to the Eighth International Church Music Congress, Rome, 1985.

[33] T. S. Eliot, "Ash Wednesday", in *The Complete Poems and Plays*, p. 67.

saints and poets of Christendom—the tremendous importance and urgency of merely sitting still . . . even among these rocks.

As one example from the literature has it, expressing that whole sense of temporal travail—in which, as Damon Runyon once amusingly remarked, "All of life is six to five against", odds just good enough, of course, to keep a fellow in the game—hope is really all that a man has on which to anchor the enterprise:

> And now we watch and struggle,
> And now we live in hope,
> And Zion in her anguish
> With Babylon must cope. . . .
>
> By hope we struggle onward
> While here we must be fed
> With milk, as tender infants,
> But there with Living Bread.

The whole life and dynamism of faith, have you noticed, are here situated within the perspective, the ambit of hope, and together they look out upon a landscape of divine never-ending love. "For anyone who is permitted", writes the late Hans Urs von Balthasar in a series of reflections on the Apostles' Creed published in the last year of his life, "to step out of his own narrow and finalized life, and into this life of God's, it seems as if vast spaces are opened up before one, taking one's breath away. Spaces into which one could hurl oneself in uttermost freedom, and these spaces are themselves freedoms that entice our love, accept it, and respond to it. . . . Life in God", he tells us, "becomes an absolute miracle".[34] This miracle, I suggest, is one upon which the whole weight of

[34] Hans Urs von Balthasar, *Credo: Meditations on the Apostles' Creed,* translated by David Kipp (New York: Crossroad, 1990).

Christian life and hope depends. If it were not so, then Christianity itself would reduce to fairy dust, the scattering and dissolution of which would make no difference whatsoever. "If Christ be not risen," warns the Apostle Paul, "then your faith is in vain . . . and we are the most miserable and abject of men."[35]

We believe, then, in the life to come, and yet we do not know this life; none of us has foreseen the shape or felt the texture of that reality to which, nevertheless, we have all been called, our own ardent desire to go there—quickened, to be sure, by God's own efficacious grace—the only proof necessary for admission. For it is not by means of scruples, to recall a line from Camus, that man will be great and thus get to Heaven. Greatness comes rather through the grace of God, like a beautiful day. Indeed, it overwhelms a man, ravishing him by its very nature. Grace, says Adrienne Von Speyr, "is the Mystery which communicates itself". The essence of the thing is that it precisely overwhelms, filling a man with the life of God. "Grace does not illuminate point by point, but irradiates like the sun. The man upon whom God lavishes himself ought to be seized by vertigo in such a way that he sees only the light of God and no longer his own limits, his own weakness."

Here we touch upon really the most fundamental feature of Christian faith, namely, its profoundly, inescapably personal character. As Joseph Ratzinger puts it in *Introduction to Christianity,* a book on which many of my students are even now cutting their theological teeth, "Christian faith is more than the option in favour of a spiritual ground to the world; its central formula is not 'I believe in something', but 'I believe in Thee'. It is the encounter with the human being Jesus, and in this encounter

---

35 See 1 Cor 15:17, 19.

it experiences the meaning of the world as a person."[36] In Christ, therefore, we encounter the sheer divine graciousness of an eternal presence:

> In his life, in the unconditional devotion of himself to men, the meaning of the world is present before us; it vouchsafes itself to us as love which loves even me and makes life worth living by this incomprehensible gift of a love free from any threat of fading away or any tinge of egotism.
>
> ... Thus faith is the finding of a "You" that bears me up and amid all the unfulfilled—and in the last resort unfulfillable—hope of human encounters gives me the promise of an indestructible love which not only longs for eternity but guarantees it. Christian faith lives on the discovery that not only is there such a thing as objective meaning, but this meaning knows me and loves me, I can trust myself to it like the child that knows all its questions answered in the "You" of its mother.[37]

It is the same child who, awakening in the night, besieged by the nameless terrors that infest the darkness, is instantly comforted by the encircling light and warmth of parental reassurance: the repeated and gentle insistence that "everything is in order, everything is all right". Only if there is finally a Heaven, the sheer promised facticity of which alone serving to banish the demons of Chaos and Old Night, only then is the mother not lying to her child (to cite the example Professor Peter Berger uses in his incisive little book *A Rumor of Angels: Modern Society and the Rediscovery of the Supernatural*).[38]

Recall once more the lines of Rilke, those incomparable

---

[36] Joseph Ratzinger, *Introduction to Christianity*, translated by J. R. Foster (San Francisco: Ignatius Press, 1990), p. 47.

[37] Ibid., p. 48.

[38] Peter L. Berger, *A Rumor of Angels: Modern Society and the Rediscovery of the Supernatural* (Garden City, N.Y.: Doubleday, 1970), pp. 52–57.

lines cited in the opening chapter from his poem "Autumn", in which everything is falling, the leaves, earth, man:

> We all are falling. This hand falls.
> And look at others: it is in them all.
>
> And yet there is One who holds this falling
> endlessly, gently in His hands.

But does he? And is there really such a place as Heaven, where this continual falling may at last and forever be held, "endlessly, gently in his hands"?

In his wonderful work on eschatology, Ratzinger writes that in all of Christian Tradition there recurs this image of Heaven, "an image linked to the natural symbolic force of what is 'high' or 'above,' in order to express that definitive completion of human existence which comes about through the perfect love towards which faith tends".[39] But is it really, finally real? For that matter, what is this faith that is supposed to ground the Christian hope we express in our longing for Heaven? Is that real or only the wish fulfillment of vain and miserable men, clutching their straws amid the encircling doom? If so, says Berger,

> the final truth would be not love but terror, not light but darkness. The nightmare of chaos, not the transitory safety of order, would be the final reality of the human situation. For, in the end, we must all find ourselves in darkness, alone with the night that will swallow us up. The face of reassuring love, bending over our terror, will then be nothing except an image of merciful illusion. In that case the last word about religion is Freud's. Religion is the childish fantasy that our parents run the universe for our benefit, a fantasy from which the mature

39 See his *Eschatology*, p. 233.

individual must free himself in order to attain whatever measure of stoic resignation he is capable of.[40]

Heaven, then, is for credulous, crippled folk who tend to hallucinate a happiness they can never have.[41]

There is a scene from Ingmar Bergman's *The Seventh Seal,* a haunting story set sometime near the end of the medieval world, in which the figure of a Christian knight—a good and honorable man, however drenched in sorrow and disillusion—finds himself in a dark confessional speaking to one he thinks is a priest but turns out to be Death; who pursues the hapless knight throughout the film (they play fitfully at chess late at night and in the early morning on windswept beaches . . . all wonderfully spooky in a dark Scandinavian way); who in this confessional scene hears the knight tell him that he wants "knowledge, not faith, not suppositions, but knowledge. I want God to stretch out his hand toward me, reveal Himself and speak to me."

Death: But He remains silent.
Knight: I call out to Him in the dark but no one seems to be there.
Death: Perhaps no one is there.
Knight: Then life is an outrageous horror. No one can live in the face of death, knowing that all is nothingness.

---

[40] Berger, *Rumor of Angels,* p. 56.

[41] There is no end of the spurious varieties of Heaven. One notes with a certain wry amusement that a famous perfume company, Calvin Klein, has recently come out with a special scent for men called *Eternity.* It goes to show that just as the Real Thing loses cachet (among the fashionable, at least, and those who frantically aspire to appear so), the counterfeit variety will rush in to fill the vacuum.

Death: Most people never reflect about either death or
the futility of life.[42]

But Christians do, and unless Christ, the world's salvation,
be risen, our prospects remain every bit as bleak and pitiless as
those that finally overtake the poor knight in Bergman's tale of
angst and despair.

Under the circumstances, the most deeply consoling statement of our Blessed Lord is the promise he gives to the
disciples: "I go and prepare a place for you . . . that where I am
you also may be."[43] But he says this the night before he is
destined to die, and so between the promise and its fulfillment
there falls the awful shadow of the Cross. Not to mention the
whole hellish weight of that Godforsakenness into whose depths
the Son of God freely descends for the world's salvation.

We thus find ourselves, do we not, somewhat in the position
of the sons of Zebedee, each of whom is most eager to sit on
either side of Christ, but of course, only *after* he has entered
upon his Glory. Jesus told them (Heaven knows with what
exasperation), "You do not know what you are asking. Can
you drink the cup I shall drink or be baptized in the same bath
of pain as I?"[44] Thus, even if it were all true, and Christ were
risen and men resolved to follow him all the way to the Cross,
how many would choose that particular platform from which
to launch out into Deep Space, this journey toward Paradise

---

[42] See Ingmar Bergman, *The Seventh Seal: A Film by Ingmar Bergman*,
translated by Lars Malmstrom and David Kushner (New York: Simon and
Schuster, 1960), p. 28.

[43] Jn 14:3.

[44] See Mk 10:35–45.

by way of Golgotha? In a word, who is *really* interested in joining Christ?[45]

Heaven's a nice place, no doubt, but nobody seems in a great rush to get there, the human race having lost, in Msgr. Ronald Knox's phrase, all relish for eternity. "It is something very astonishing", observes von Balthasar, "that all of the ancient peoples reflected in so many diverse ways on the 'hereafter' while modern people are scarcely interested in the matter. It is as though their wings had been clipped; as though the spiritual organ for the transcendent had atrophied."[46]

This quite extraordinary aberration, it seems to me, is the result of two things, two influences that together work to undermine genuine hope in the reality of Heaven: first, the seductions of secularity, the sheer weight and delectation of which engender a kind of forgetfulness of being (Lewis calls it an "Evil Enchantment"). The fact of worldly preoccupation induces a certain amnesia concerning the Last Things, most especially that eschatological horizon in which being is carried to triumphant completion and history to its destiny. What is under attack here is the purpose of life understood and lived out against a backdrop ultimately beyond life. And, point two, the frequent and astounding insipidity of so much that passes

[45] "Therefore, since we are surrounded by so great a cloud of witnesses, let us also lay aside every weight, and sin which clings so closely, and let us run with perseverance the race that is set before us, looking to Jesus the pioneer and perfecter of our faith, who for the joy that was set before Him endured the cross, despising the shame, and is seated at the right hand of the throne of God" (Heb 12:1–2). In other words, are we really all that anxious to enlist in a race whose front runner seemingly came to such a bad end?

[46] See his article "Eternal Life and the Human Condition", *Communio* 18 (Spring 1991): 4.

for the pleasures and joys of Heaven—call it the sentimental-
ization of Paradise: that too works against an interest, both
abiding and real, in anyone wanting to go there.

So, on the one hand, we find ourselves, as Aldous Huxley
once put it, in a world wrapped in cellophane, indeed, a world
deeply, fiercely hostile to the grammar and the poetry of the
transcendent. And what is so completely astonishing about it is
that no one appears to have missed the music or seems terribly
anxious to cut through the cellophane. Why is it, to sound the
great hymnal of Christian hope—that is, "In Heaven our joy
will be to sing eternally: may Jesus Christ be praised"—why is
it that so many seem so indifferent to rehearsing the Song?
Could it be, as Professor Berger writes, that "with the onset of
secularization . . . the divine fullness began to recede, until the
point was reached when the empirical sphere became both
all-encompassing and perfectly closed in upon itself. At that
point man was truly alone in reality"?[47]

We are thus, he concludes, in a situation where God and the
transcendent have been reduced to the status of a rumor, a kind
of conspiratorial whisper among a furtive few who increasingly
find themselves surrounded by massive, all-encompassing structures of secularity. It is a situation in which man is literally
gasping for breath. In fact, to recall Danielou's warning issued
many years ago, it is precisely one of spiritual asphyxiation, the
condition of man left to himself, deprived of the energies of
God.

The Anglican theologian E. L. Mascall has likewise diag-
nosed the malaise. In his book *The Christian Universe*, he
writes:

> Our present age is radically secularized. . . . The vast majority
> of men and women today organize their lives on the assump-

tion that the only realities of which they need to take account are those that are perceived by their senses in the brief span of time that lies between their conception in their mother's womb and their death on the motorway or in the hospital bed. This carries with it two consequences: first, that there is nothing after death that we need bother about, neither Heaven, Hell, nor Purgatory; secondly, that there is nothing during this life that we need bother about except the things of this world, neither God nor angels nor devils, neither prayer nor grace nor holiness.[48]

What a bloody impoverishment to inflict on men! How vastly different from the circumstances that once characterized our ancestors' lives, men and women who despite conditions of fearful superstition were yet steeped in that piety toward the constitution of being that lies at the heart of all natural religion. "Worshipping snakes or trees, . . . devils rather than nothing: crying for life beyond life, for ecstasy not of the flesh", as T. S. Eliot puts it in one of his poems.[49]

They remain, therefore, deeply kindred to Christian thought and practice in ways in which our secular neighbors are not. The merest savage dancing madly about the entrails of a disemboweled turkey in obscene search of God is surely a more sympathetic figure than some fussy-minded, post-Christian shopper, looking for turkey drumsticks under a cellophane wrapper amid the plastic perfections of a suburban supermarket. At least the savage is in search of authentic liberation from sin and death, which neither the post-Christian nor his vaunted machinery can confer. It is this terrible craving of the pagan soul for reassurance about its own essential immortality—the

---

[48] E. L. Mascall, *The Christian Universe: The Boyle Lectures, 1965* (London: Darton, Longman & Todd, 1966), pp. 14–15.

[49] See his *Choruses from "The Rock"*, VII.

possibility of real purification from sin and iniquity; the aboriginal, consuming hunger for wholeness, for atonement with itself and God, the world, and others—that fundamentally describes the persisting, immemorial conditions for the very existence of religion itself.

It is a word, incidentally, that comes from the Latin, meaning to bind oneself back or to be bound to some source or origin in being . . . *religare*, a word that necessarily implies some recognition of contingency, of dependency upon grace, upon God.

And so there is something profoundly healthy about paganism; it is, for all its grotesquerie, at least a human thing, an expression quintessentially human and honest because it begins with belief. Man is a being born to believe, and no pagan soul can abide the absence of God's presence from the world. The pagan is driven thus to hallow the whole universe to ensure that the sacred not disappear, that all the significant moments of a man's life—birth, marriage, coming of age, death—be invested with numinous importance. Paganism, I am saying, is a natural and good and eminently human impulse, which for all its distortion and abuse is worth defending because here, at least, is something to which human hope might anchor its energy and idealism, riveted upon some future state of real and lasting happiness. In short, because it is healthy and human enough to hope for Heaven, paganism is something we can build upon, a thing God's grace may perfect, yes, even unto glory.

The other impediment, of course, to any lively curiosity about the world to come—not to mention this strange unnatural reluctance of so many of us actually to get up and go there—is that too often the images we have been given on which to hang the heavenly hat have been sentimentalized, and thus they remain too cloyingly oppressive for men ever to bother about. "If I had to sum up the crowds I have talked to on street corners in the last forty years," Frank Sheed reminisced near the end of a life marked by an extraordinary amount of evangelism, "I would say that practically nobody wants to go to Heaven. I don't mean that I myself am at this moment anxious to leave this world and be on my way to the next. But all the same I do see Heaven as a place of great joys. Most people apparently don't."[50] The reason is that for most people the only idea they have of Heaven is the everlastingly boring one of men and women seated forever on a cloud playing harps and shouting Hosannas. Imagine, if you can bear it, the prospect of an eternal guitar Mass, accompanied by the Saint Louis Jesuits singing, "Yahweh, I Know You Are Near". Such things reduce eternal life to a sort of "supertechnicolor church service"—a pretty miserable compensation for all the sins they fear they shall have to give up in order to get there.

Sheed, for example, recounts the case of the man who asked a speaker in Hyde Park, "Will there be toilets in Heaven?" Apparently the poor fellow was "unable to bear the thought of an eternity without a wall to write on".[51] In any case, the speaker answered that there would be only if there were waste matter to be eliminated, concerning which he had no information. And then, there were those early Christians who gave up their wives in the hope of receiving a hundredfold in Heaven. Weren't they in for a shock!

The point is, we've managed to trivialize enormously the life of the Blessed in Heaven. Many of us, alas, seem never to

---

[50] F. J. Sheed, *Death into Life: A Conversation* (New York: Arena Letters, 1977), p. 92.
[51] Ibid.

have improved upon the imagery of very young children, who associate Heaven with that place where, as one resourceful child of seven put it, "You don't have to do homework unless your teacher is there, too." Or the girl who thought of Heaven as God taking care of her just like her mother, only he never yells or makes you straighten up your room. I will spare the reader the details of what my two oldest sons think the joys of Heaven consist, because they often involve the exclusion of their sisters.[52]

This brings us finally to the heart of the matter, to that christological center whence all the arteries of our common faith circulate in their movement to encompass and embrace the world, to unite all things in him whose Word bespeaks Salvation from beginning to end.

What is it, really, that gives rise to my longing to live forever, to savor unending joy and delight? It is not, says Ratzinger, "the isolated I, but the experience of the other, of love. Love wills eternity for the beloved and therefore for itself."[53] Immortality, he says in effect, does not belong to me but depends rather on my being-in-relation to others, the bond of which is love. That is what constitutes eternity and makes it meaningful.

"This abidingness," Ratzinger continues, "which gives life and can fulfill it, is truth. It is also love. Man can therefore live forever, because he is able to have a relationship with that which gives the eternal . . . the truth and love that we call

---

[52] One of whom, by the way, would often ask with that look of wide-eyed wonder that so endears us to the very young, "When will God open the clouds, Papa, and come down?" How I wish I knew so that I might have told her!

[53] Ratzinger, *Eschatology,* p. 259.

'God' give man eternity."[54] This is how, it seems to me, we are to understand the moving statement once made by Gabriel Marcel: "To love a person means to say: You will not die."[55]

And if, as Mother Church tells us, Heaven essentially depends on being in Christ, then this being in Christ necessarily includes a co-being with all those who, taken together, make up the total Body of Christ. "Heaven is a stranger to isolation. It is the open society of the communion of saints, and in this way the fulfillment of all human communion."[56] The bliss of Heaven, in other words, includes both dimensions, that is, the immediate vision and love of God (vertical) and the knowledge and love of all others in God (horizontal). Here the Church's *Catechism* is wonderfully plainspoken: "Heaven is the blessed community of all who are perfectly incorporated into Christ."[57]

---

[54] "Plato had recognized that immortality can only come from that which is immortal, from the truth. He saw that for human beings hope for eternal life is based on a relation to the truth. But in the last resort, the truth is an abstraction. When, in the event, someone entered the world who could say of himself, 'I am the Truth' (John 14:6), the significance of Plato's assertion was fundamentally altered" (p. 259).

[55] Earlier on, Ratzinger adverts to "that quite primordial sensation which Nietzsche expressed in the words, 'All joy wills eternity, wills deep, deep eternity.'" And commenting upon the fact that there are moments, and meanings attached to them, that ought never to pass away (that they do, he says, "is the real sadness of human existence"), he goes on to ask, "How can we describe that moment in which we experience what life truly is? It is the moment of love, a moment which is simultaneously the moment of truth when life is discovered for what it is. The desire for immortality does not arise from the fundamentally unsatisfying enclosed existence of the isolated self, but from the experience of love, of communion, of the Thou. It issues from that call which the Thou makes upon the I, and which the I returns. The discovery of life entails going beyond the I, leaving it behind. It happens only when one ventures along the path of self-abandonment, letting oneself fall into the hands of another" (p. 94).

[56] Ratzinger, *Eschatology,* p. 235.

[57] CCC, 1026.

Our capacity finally to enter and thus experience Heaven will depend on the extent of our willingness to receive and to give love. If God's love lies at the origin of his reckless invitation to us to come home to Paradise—the person whom God loves will never pass away!—then of course it must follow that the love we give, tossed with Christ-like abandon upon the least and the lost (alas, more often than not, the neighbor next door, the parent or child down the hall, the wife on the same sofa . . . so seldom the remote and sentimentalized victim across the sea), will be the actual permission slip we need to get in. "Heaven, then, is none other than the certainty that God is great enough to have room even for us insignificant mortals."[58] Provided, of course, we too are willing to extend the same courtesy to others.[59]

Let me now bring all this to a close with the figure of Dante, the sheer grandeur and reach of whose imaginative genius is that he succeeded in piercing the very dome of Heaven and the Face of God, where, in a kind of blissful

---

[58] "But God never passes away, and we all exist because He loves us, because He brought us into existence by His creative act. His love is the foundation of our eternity. One whom God loves never passes away." Ratzinger, *Co-Workers of the Truth*, p. 376.

[59] In *Dare We Hope*, Balthasar recounts the wonderfully instructive story Dostoevski tells in *The Brothers Karamazov*, about the wicked old woman in Hell, who tenaciously clings to the onion she had once given to a poor beggar (it was the only decent thing she'd ever done in her life), which is now being drawn up out of the lake of fire by an angel holding onto it. Observing this, others try and take hold of the onion, too, "so that they could be pulled out along with her. But the woman was wicked, very wicked, and kicked them away, screaming, 'Only I am to be pulled out, not you; it is my onion and not yours.' As soon as she had said that," reports Dostoevski in his parable, "the little plant broke in two, and the woman fell back into the lake and remains there burning to this very day" (p. 57).

swoon, gazing upon the very Godhead itself, he tells us something of what we may expect to see on the other side of death, the very threshold of eternal life. And that, we may be sure, is the operative word here: sight, vision: God seen as a single indivisible point of light, surrounded by so many Seraphic concentric circles of light, as Dante tells us in canto 30 of the "Paradiso", and as Saint John himself confirms in his first Letter.[60] In canto 33 of the "Paradiso", then, the final movement of *La Divina Comedia,* Dante writes:

> So my mind, held in complete suspense,
> Gazed fixedly, motionless and intent,
> And always as if on fire with the gazing.
>
> In that light a man becomes such
> That it is impossible he should turn away
> Ever to look upon any other thing.
>
> Because the good, which is the object of the will,
> Is there in its entirety; and outside it
> There is some defect in what there is perfect.
>
> My language now will be more inadequate,
> Even for what I remember, than would that
> Of a child still bathing his tongue at the breast.
>
> Not that there was more than a simple appearance
> In the living light which I gazed upon
> And which is always as it always has been;
>
> It was my sight which was growing stronger
> As I was looking; so what looked like one
> Worked on me as I myself changed.

[60] See 1 Jn 1:5.

In the profundity of the clear substance
Of the deep light, appeared to me three circles
Of three colours and equal circumference;

And the first seemed to be reflected by the second,
As a rainbow by a rainbow, and the third,
Seemed like a flame breathed equally from both.

O how my speech falls short, how faint it is
For my conception! And for what I saw
It is not enough to say that I say little.

O eternal light, existing in yourself alone,
Alone knowing yourself; and who, known to yourself
And knowing, love and smile upon yourself!

That circle which, conceived in this manner,
Appeared in you as a reflected light,
When my eyes examined it rather more,

Within itself, and in its own colour,
Seemed to be painted with our effigy;
And so absorbed my attention altogether.

Like a geometer who sets himself
To square the circle, and is unable to think
Of the formula he needs to solve the problem,

So was I faced with this new vision:
I wanted to see how the image could fit the circle
And how could it be that that was where it was;[61]

---

[61] In other words, the startling, unheard-of convergence of God and Man in Christ; what Ratzinger in his *Introduction to Christianity* breath-catchingly calls "the absolutely staggering alliance of *logos* and *sarx,* of meaning and a single historical Figure" (see p. 141). It is of course into this mysterious ontology, the very furnace of the God-Man's life and love, that the poet Dante is taken.

But that was not a flight for my wings:
Except that my mind was struck by a flash
In which what it desired came to it.

At this point high imagination failed;
But already my desire and my will
Were being turned like a wheel, all at one speed,

By the love which moves the sun and the other stars.[62]

---

[62] See Dante, *The Divine Comedy,* translated by C. H. Sisson (Chicago: Regnery Gateway, 1981), pp. 498–99.